LARGE PRINT

COLORING BOOK

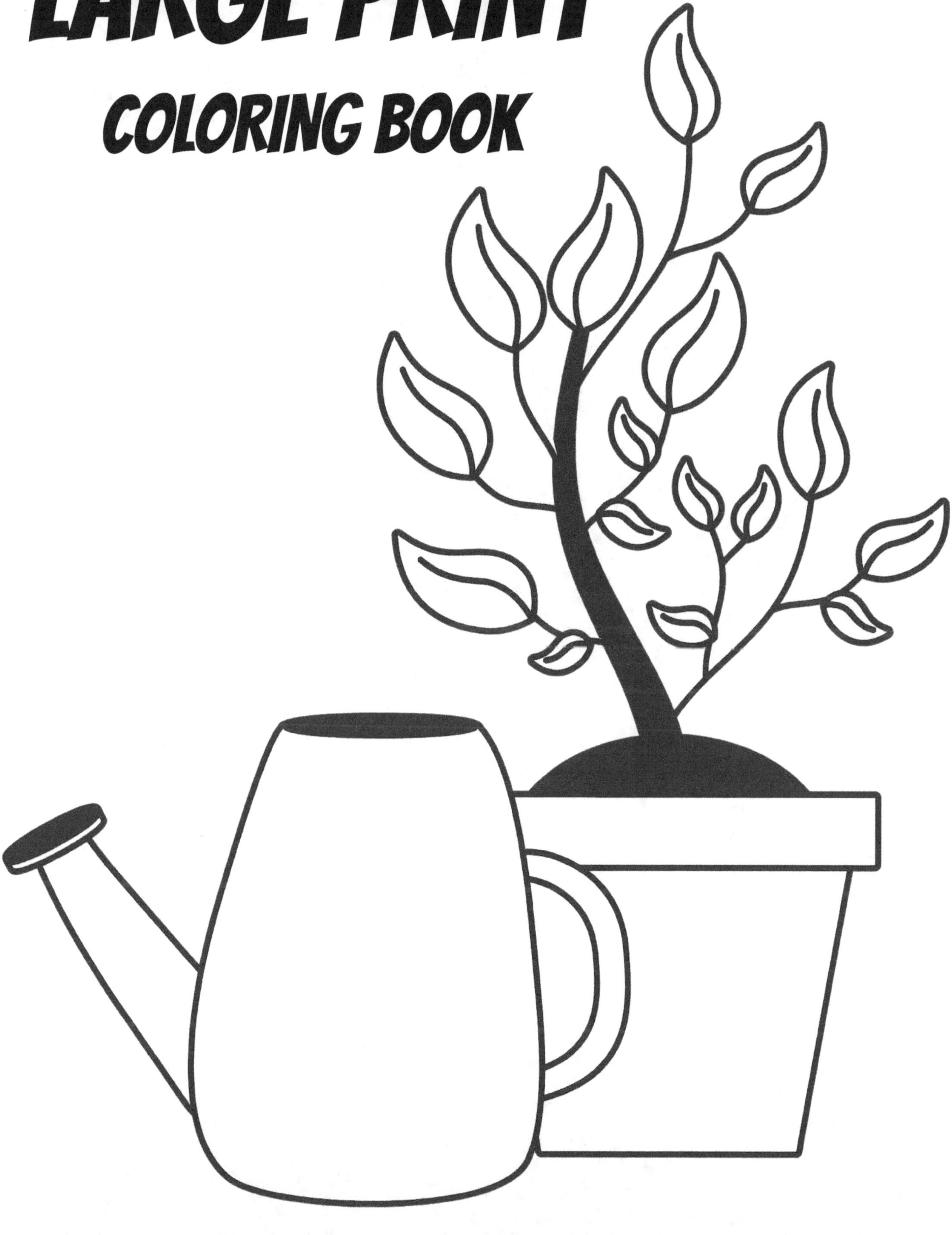

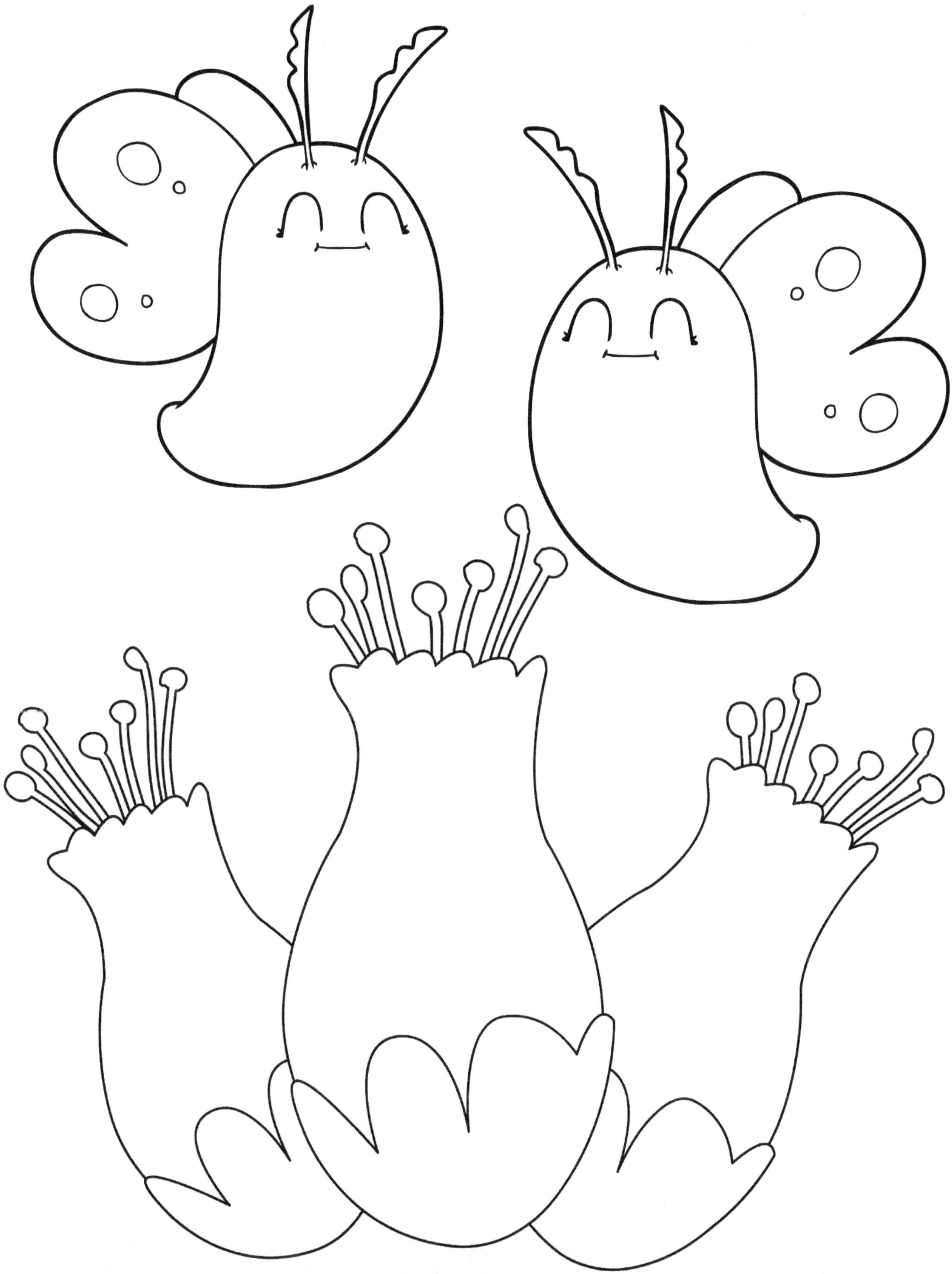

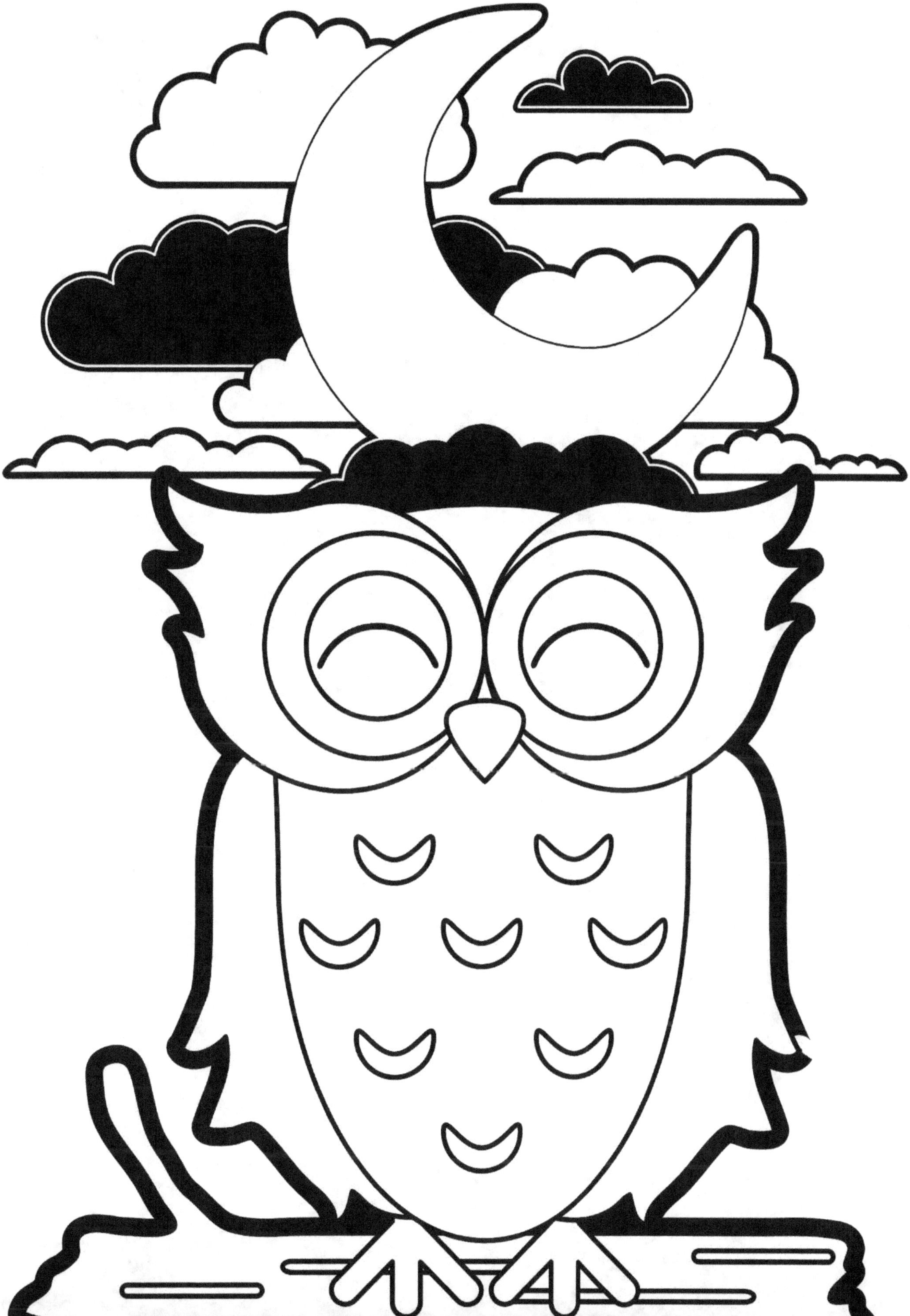

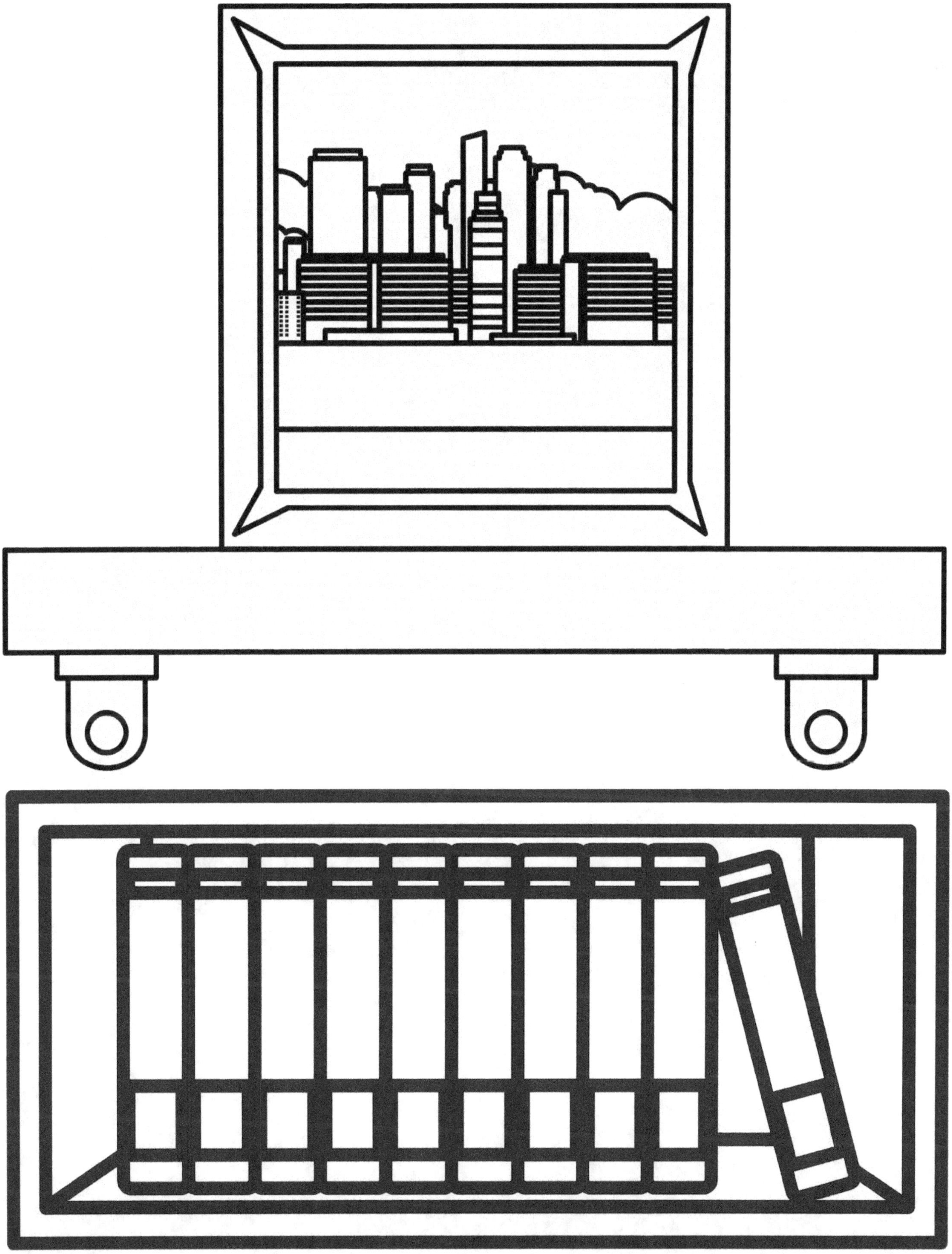

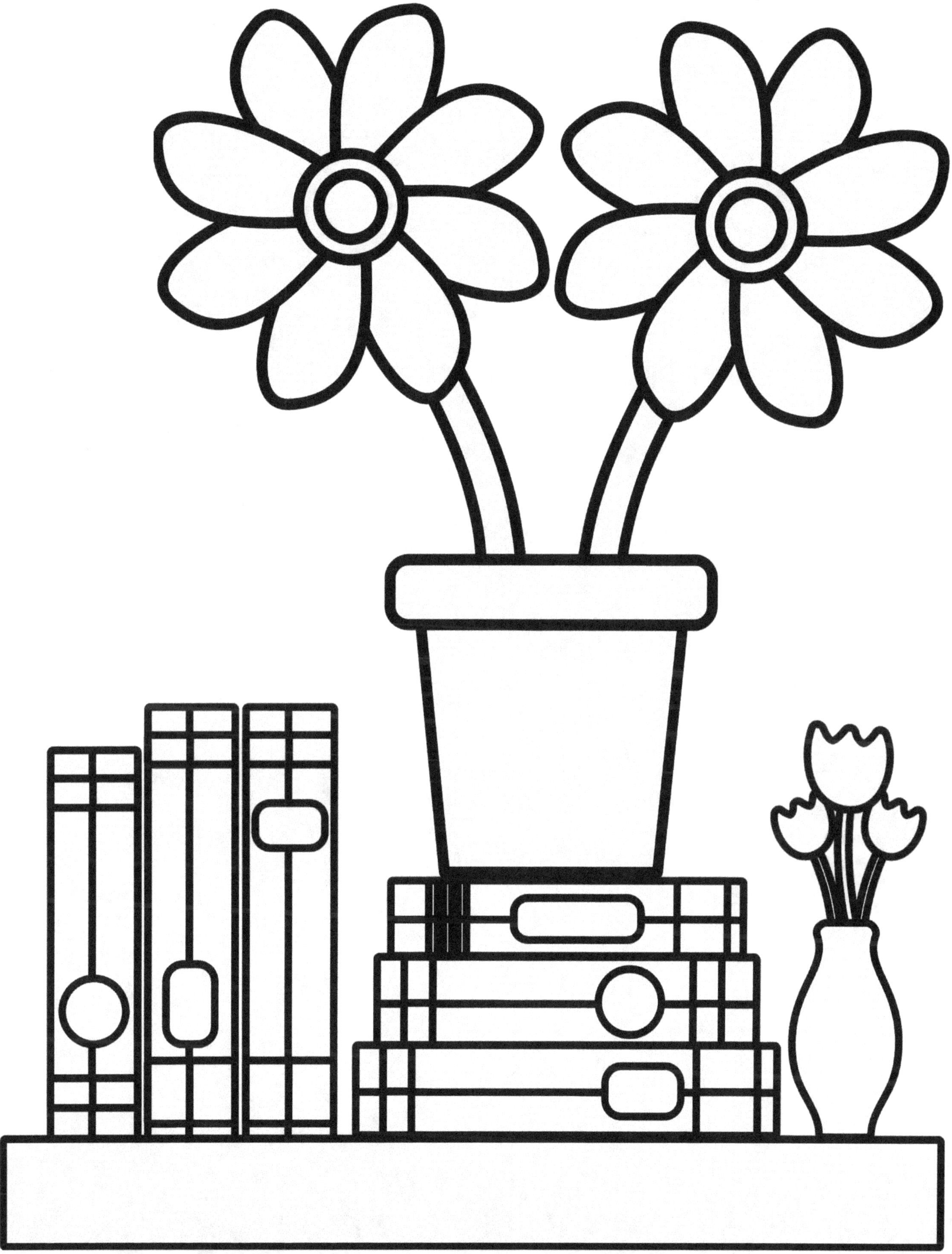

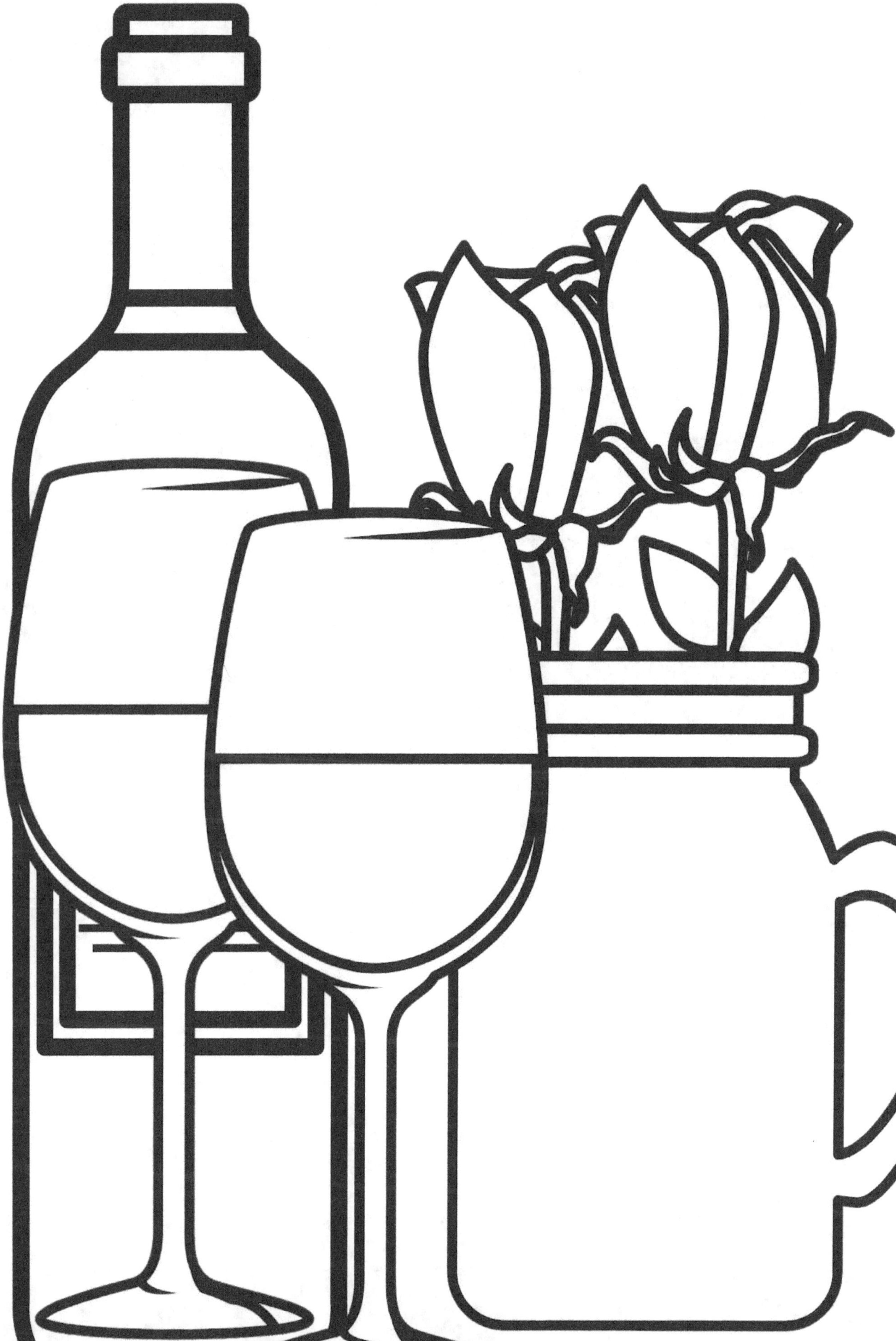

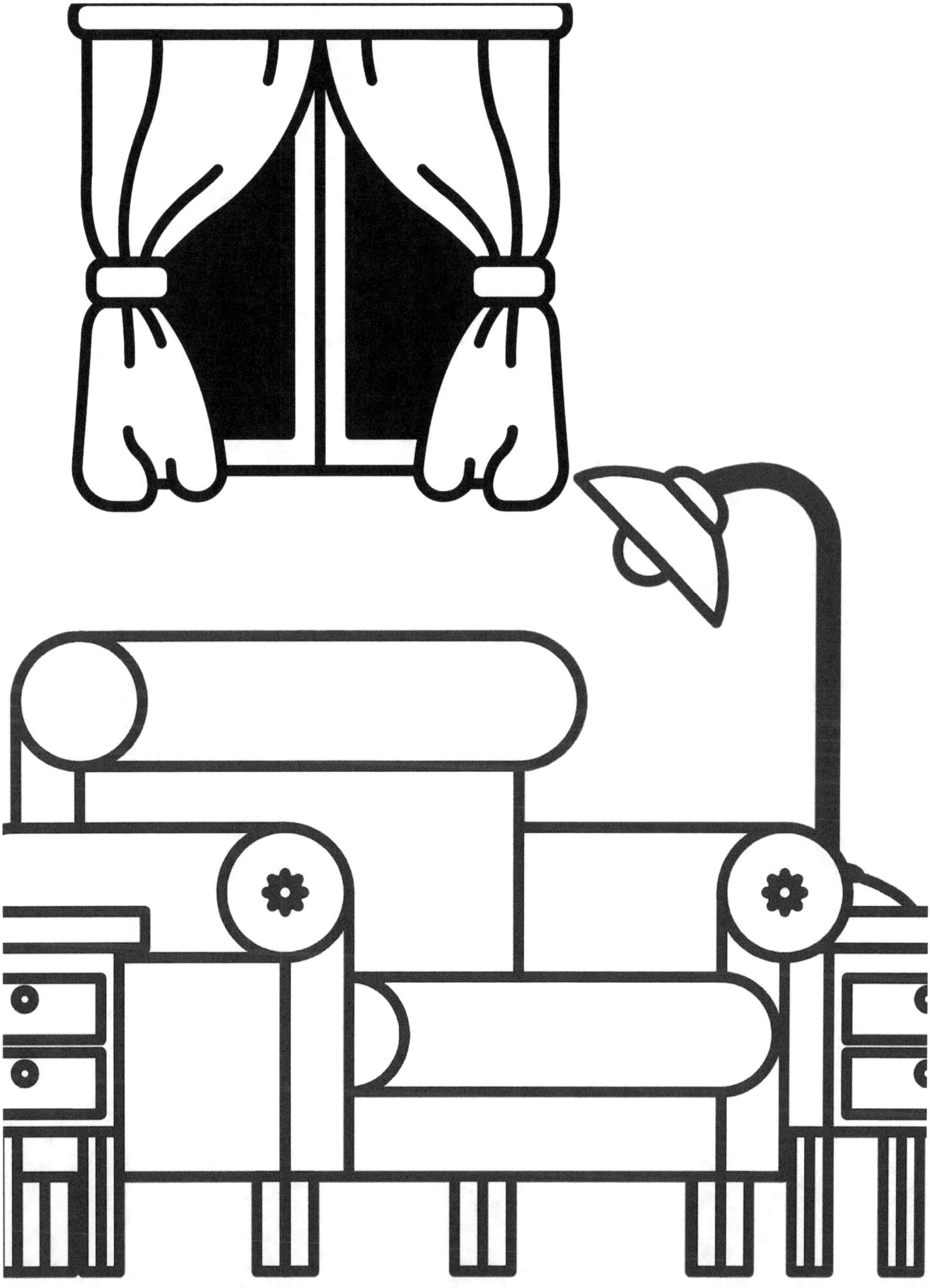

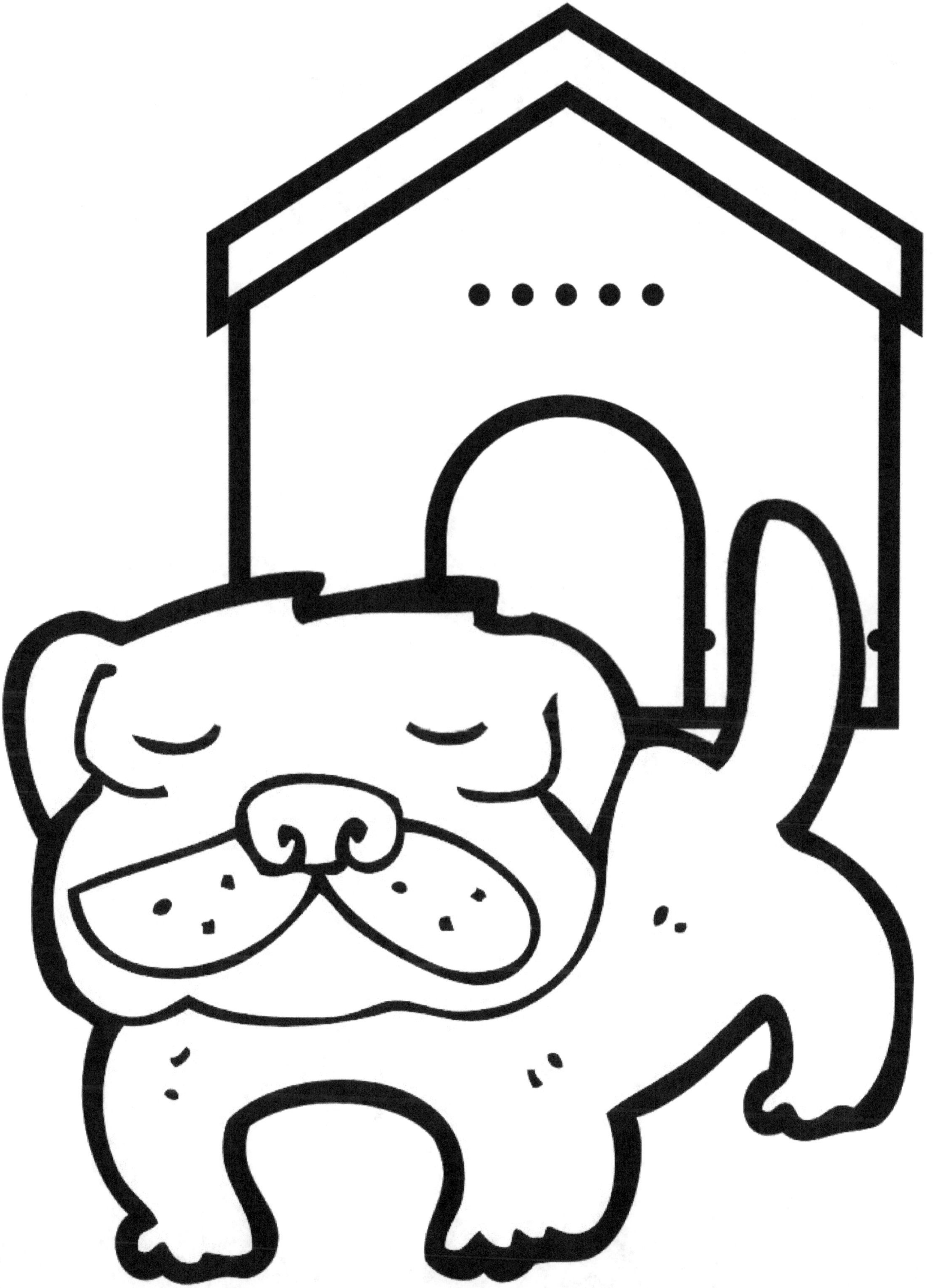

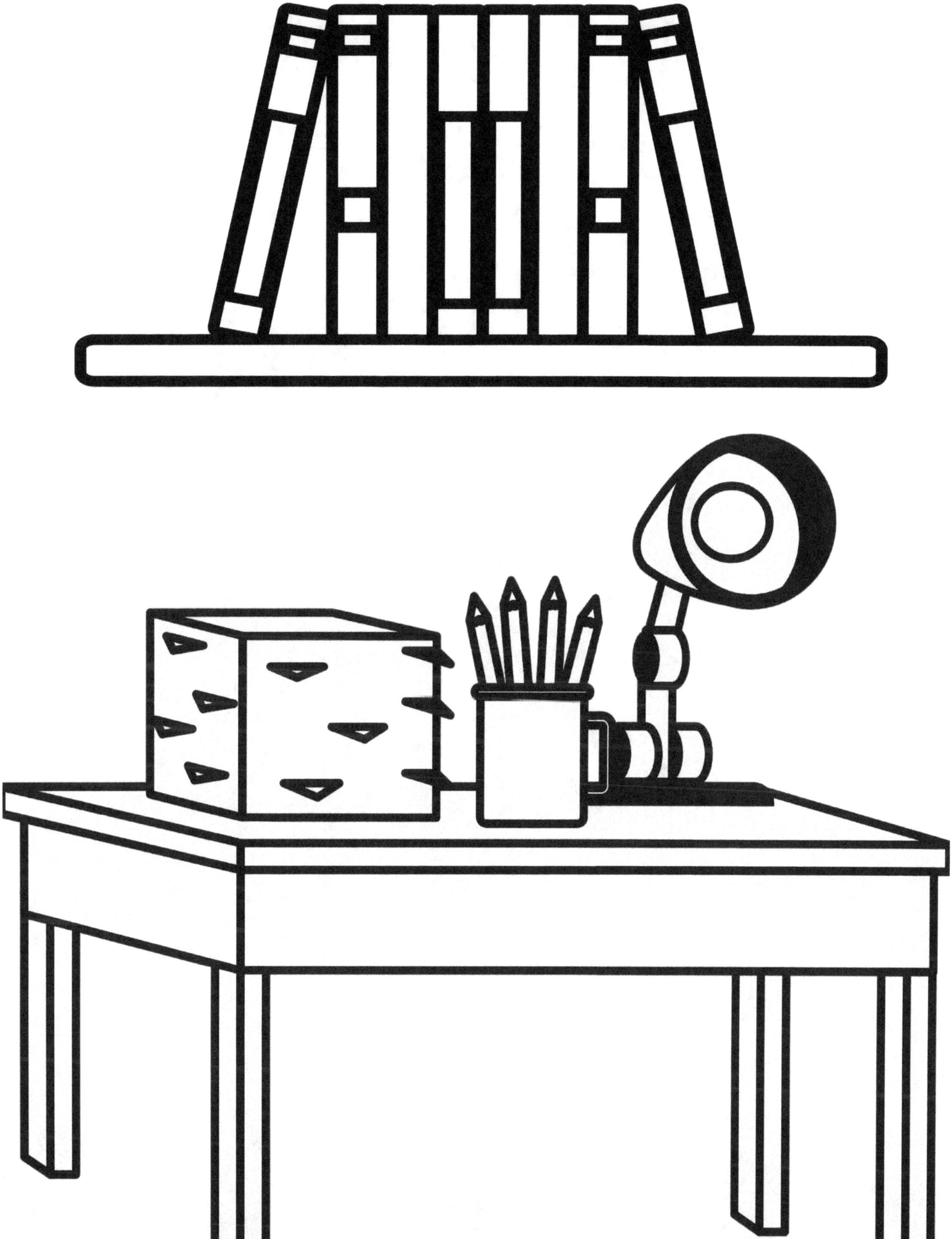

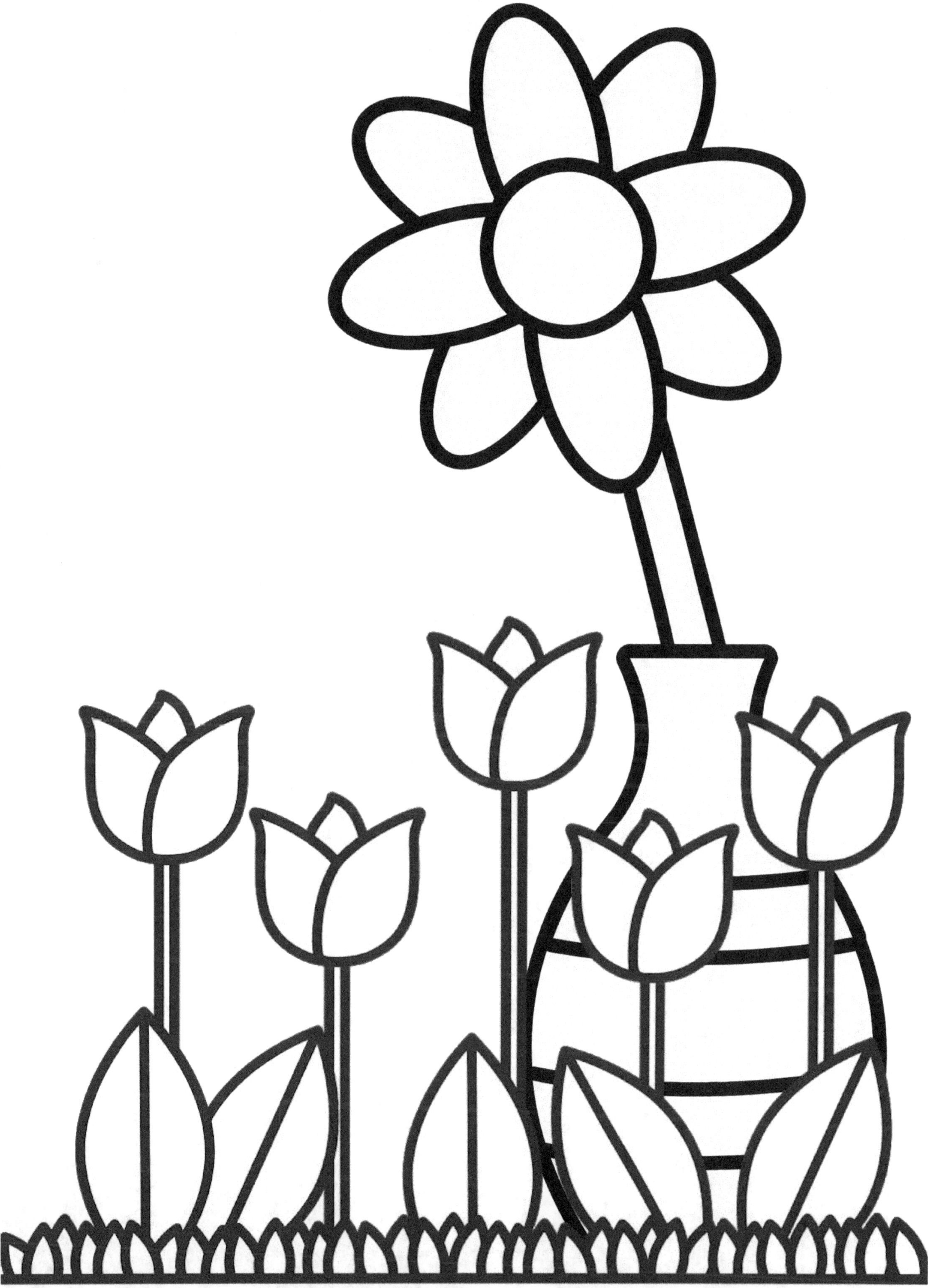

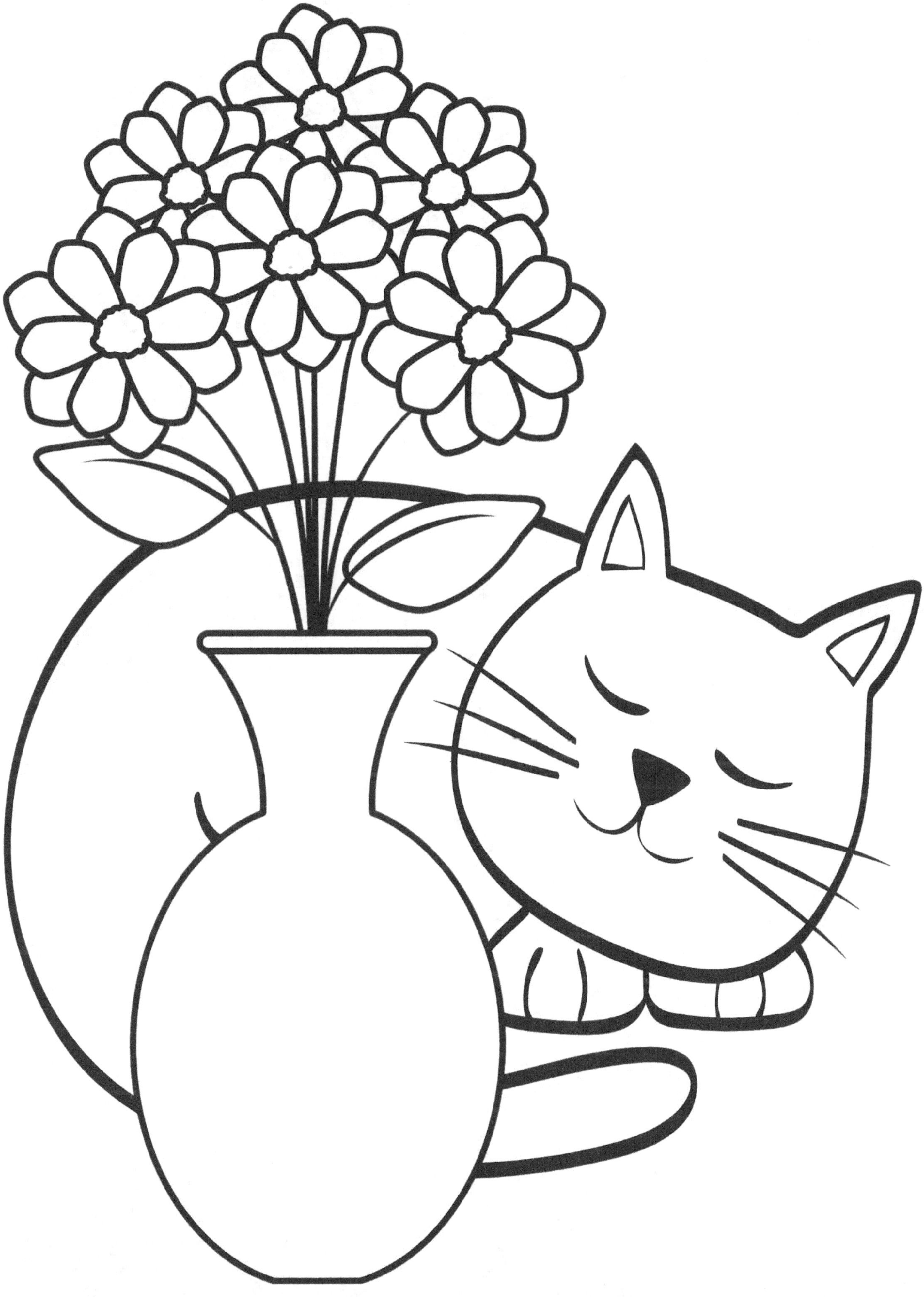

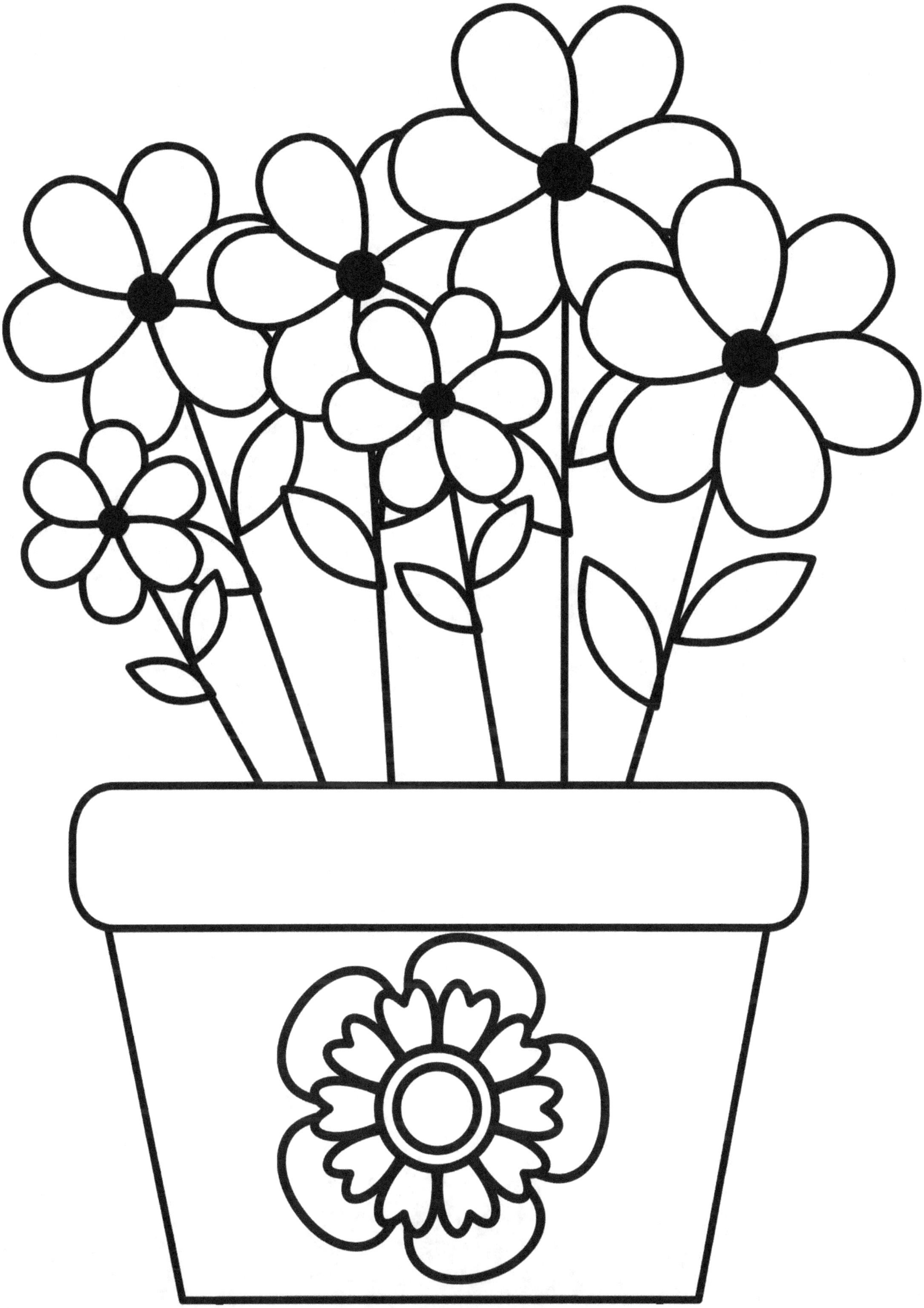

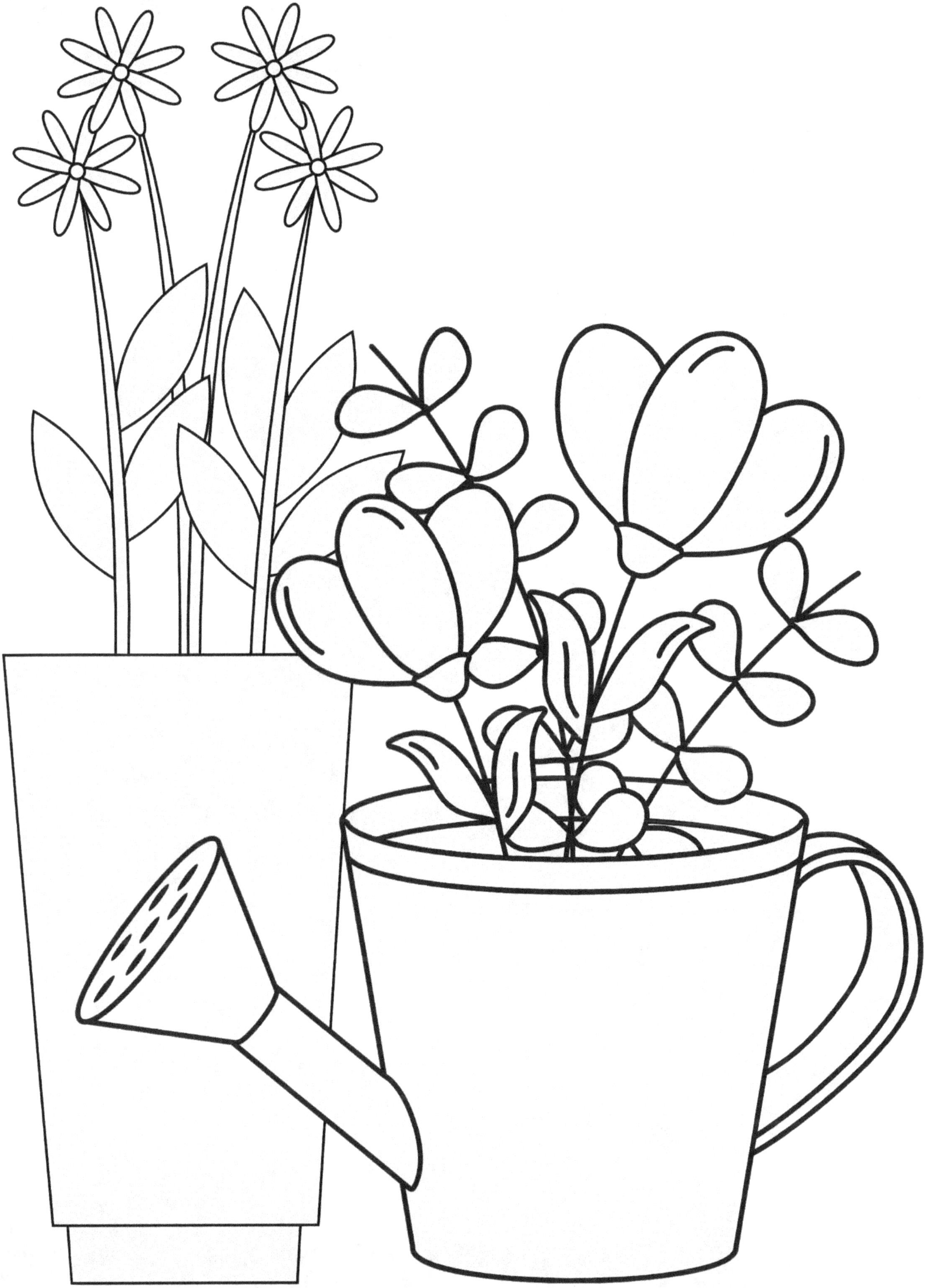

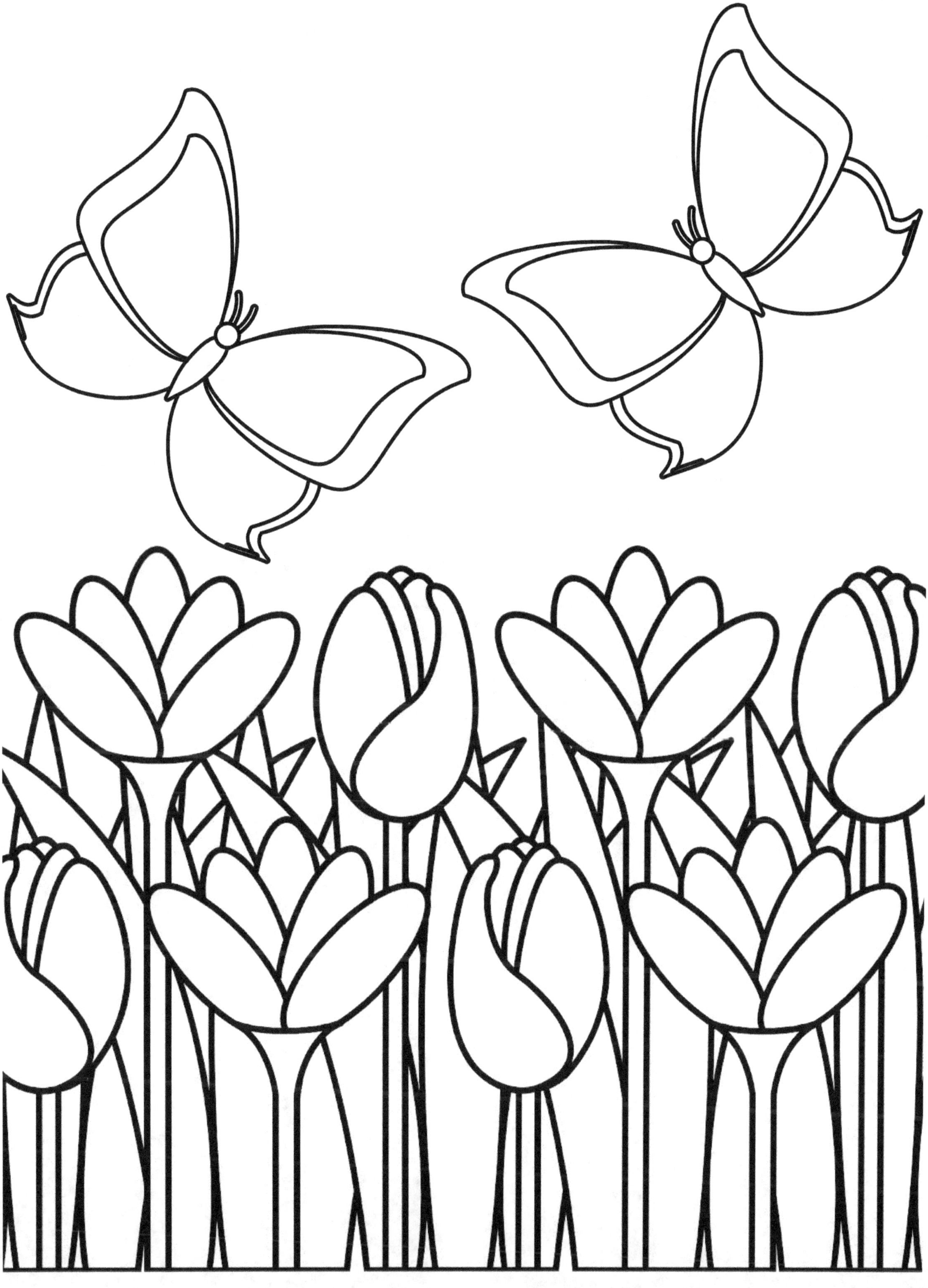

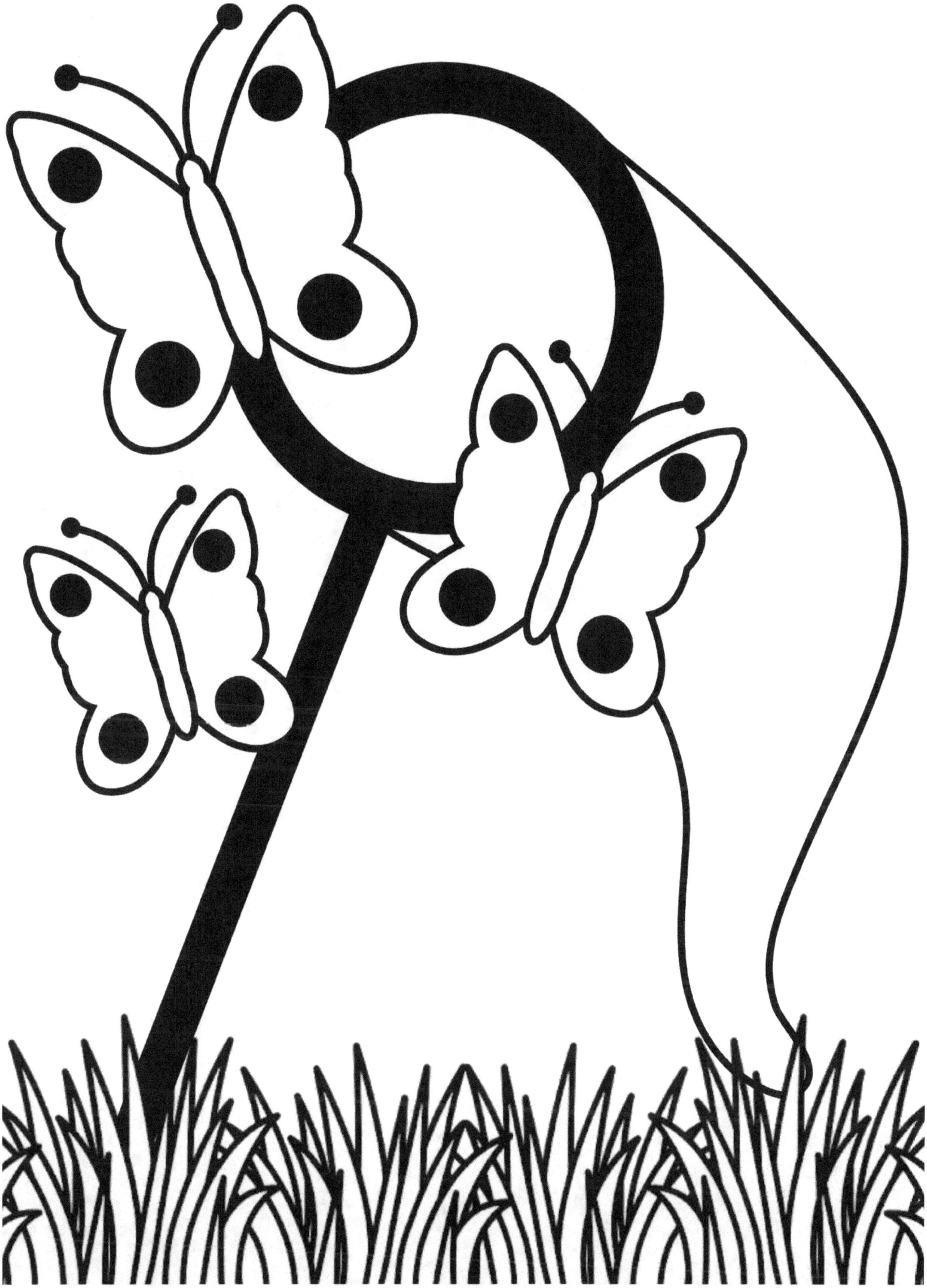

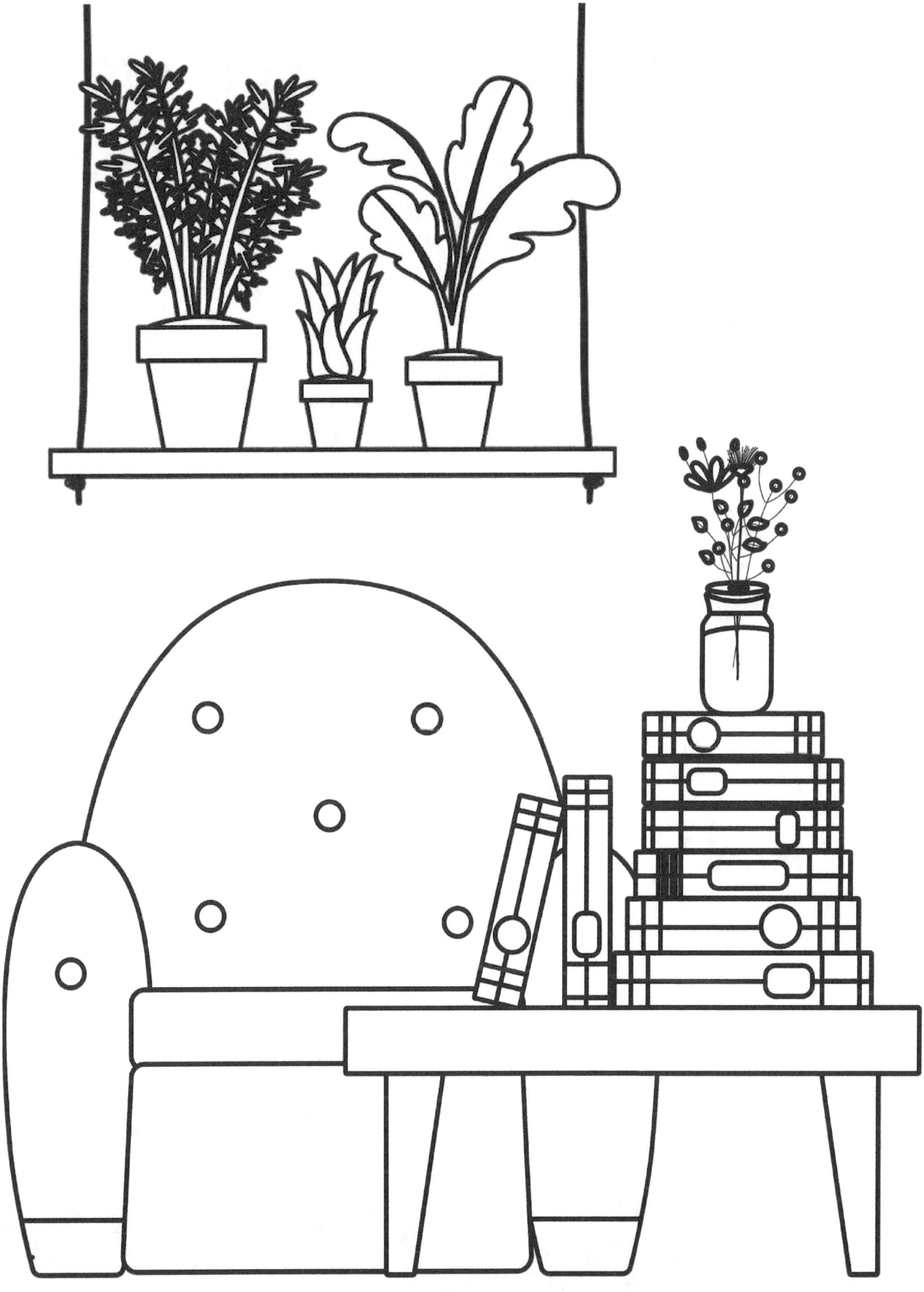

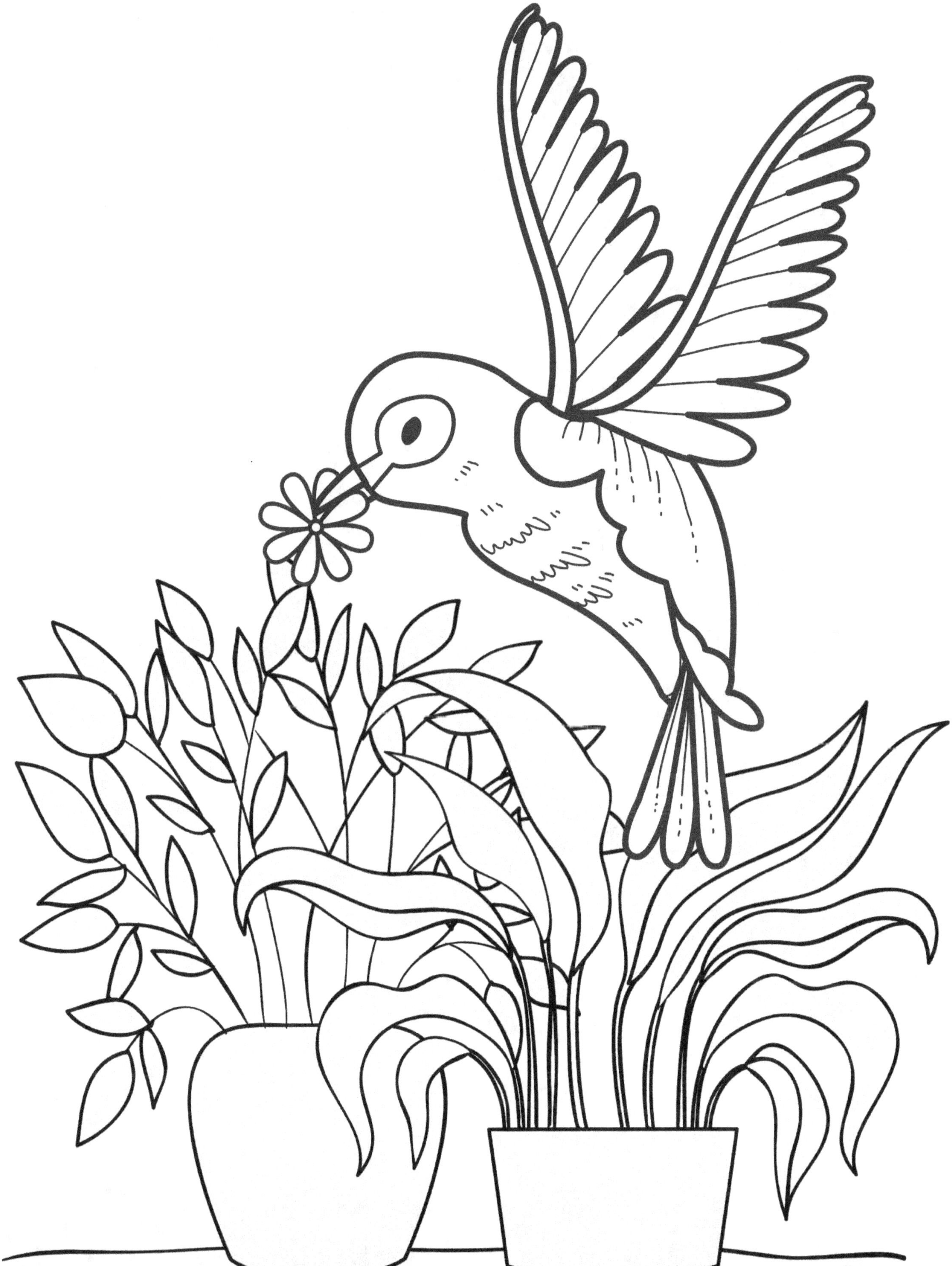

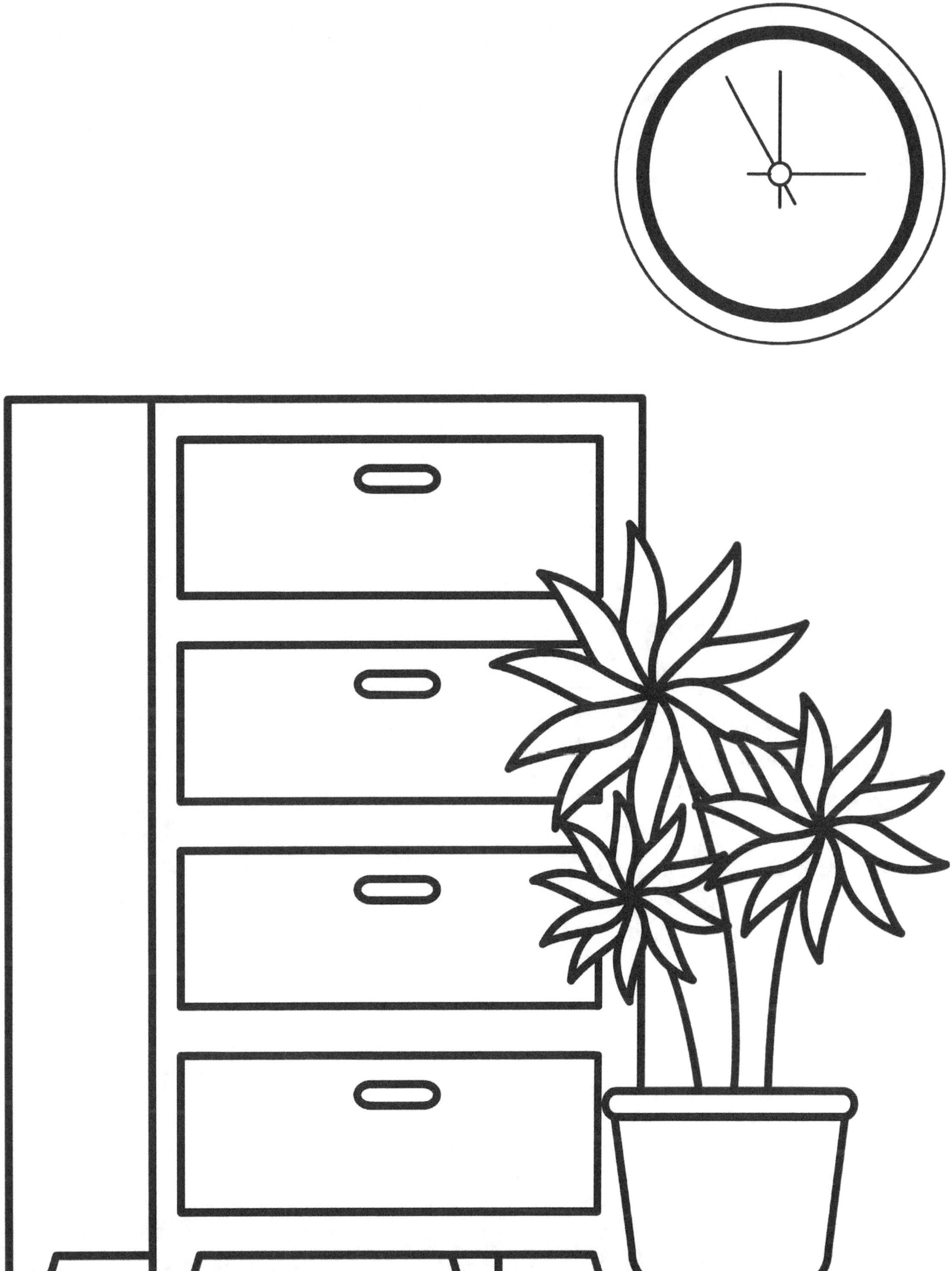

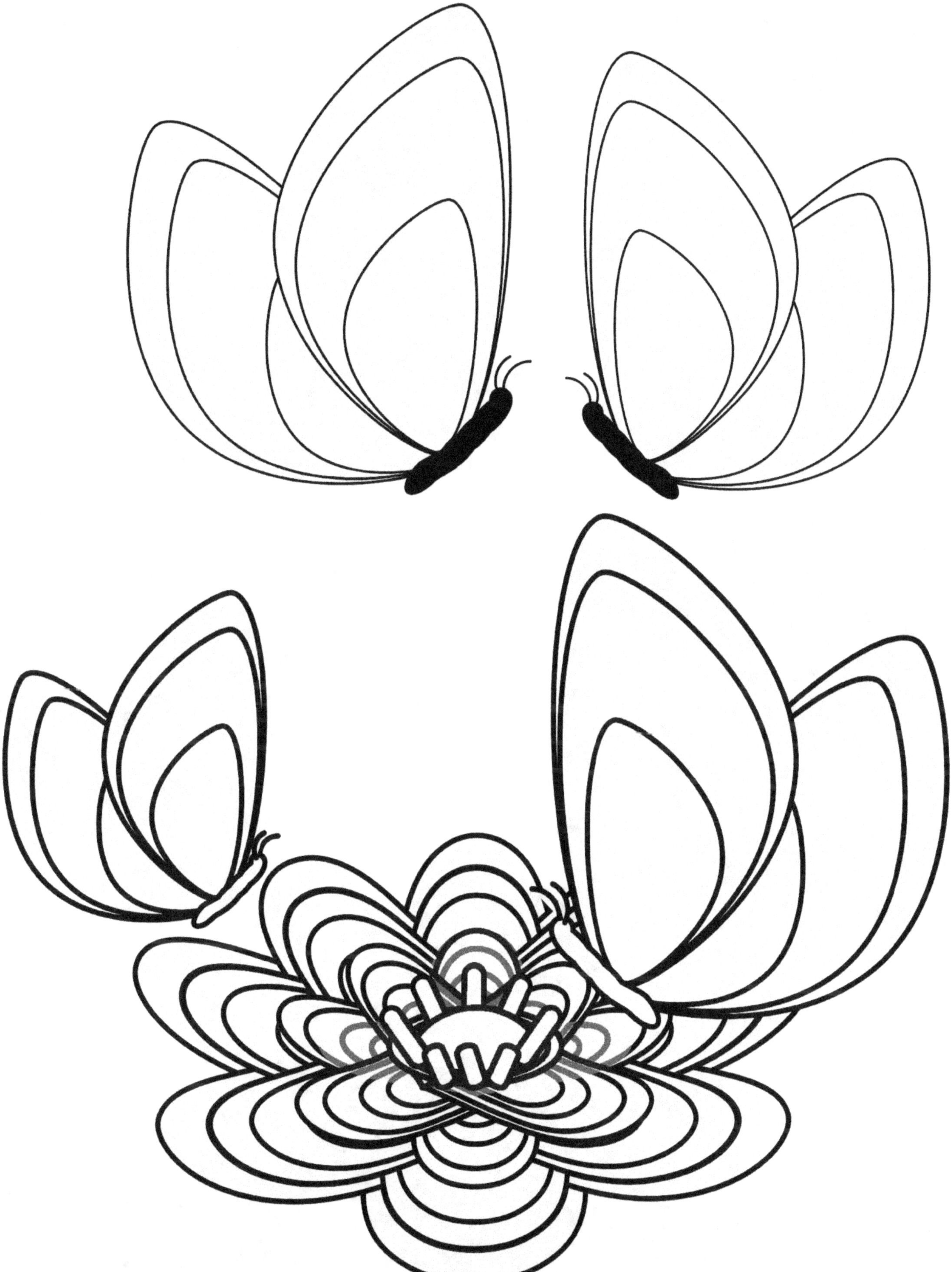

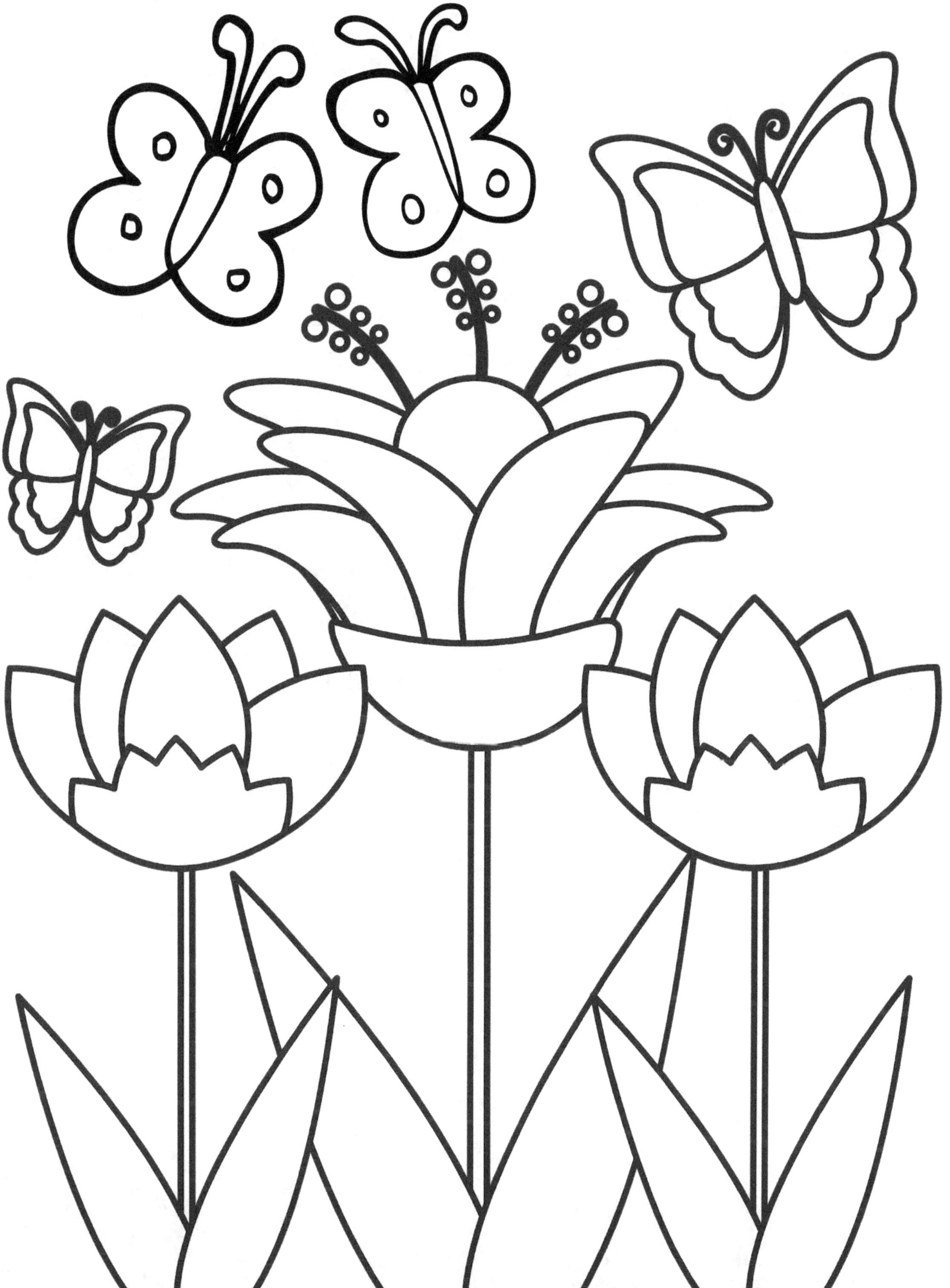

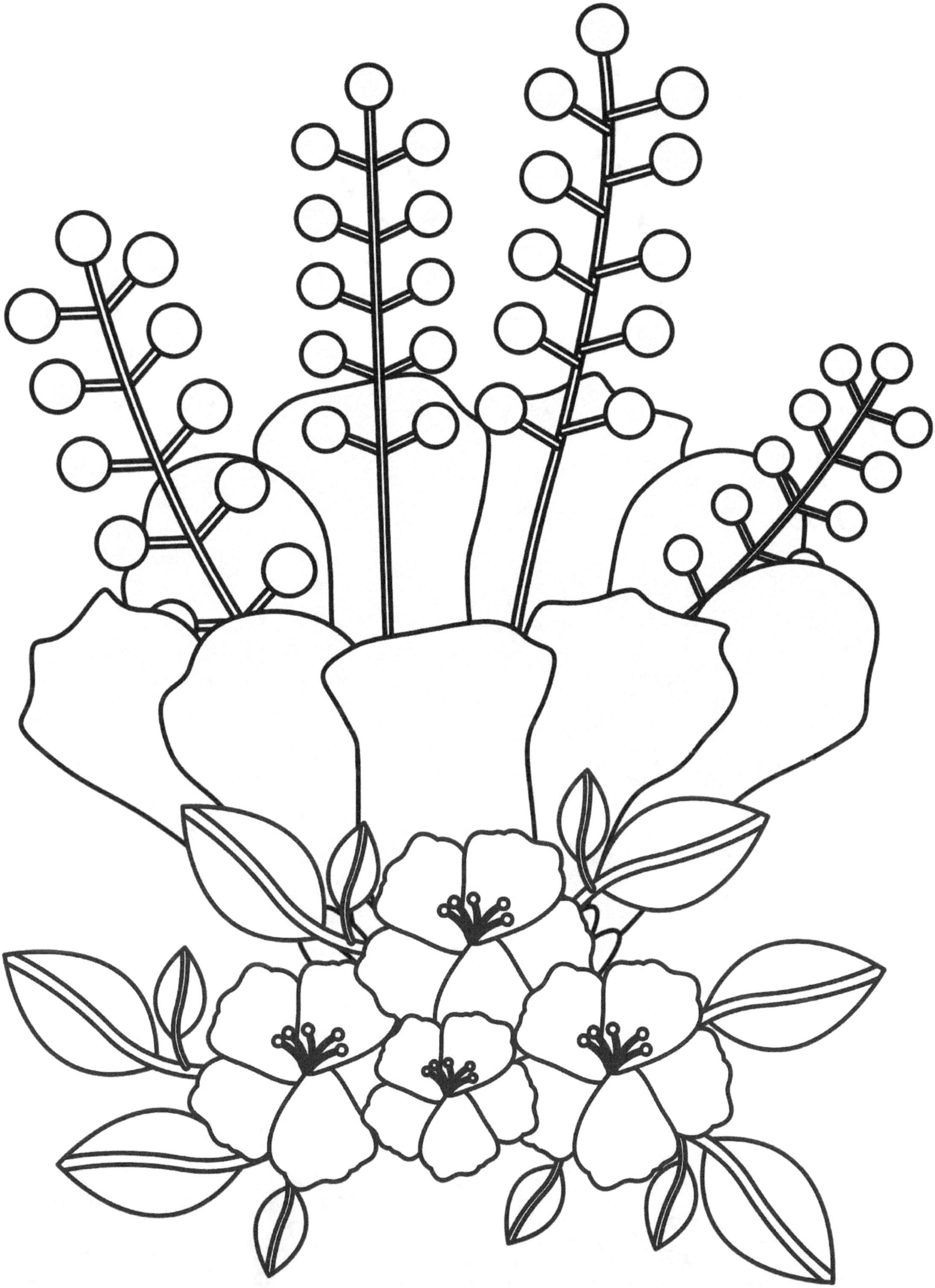

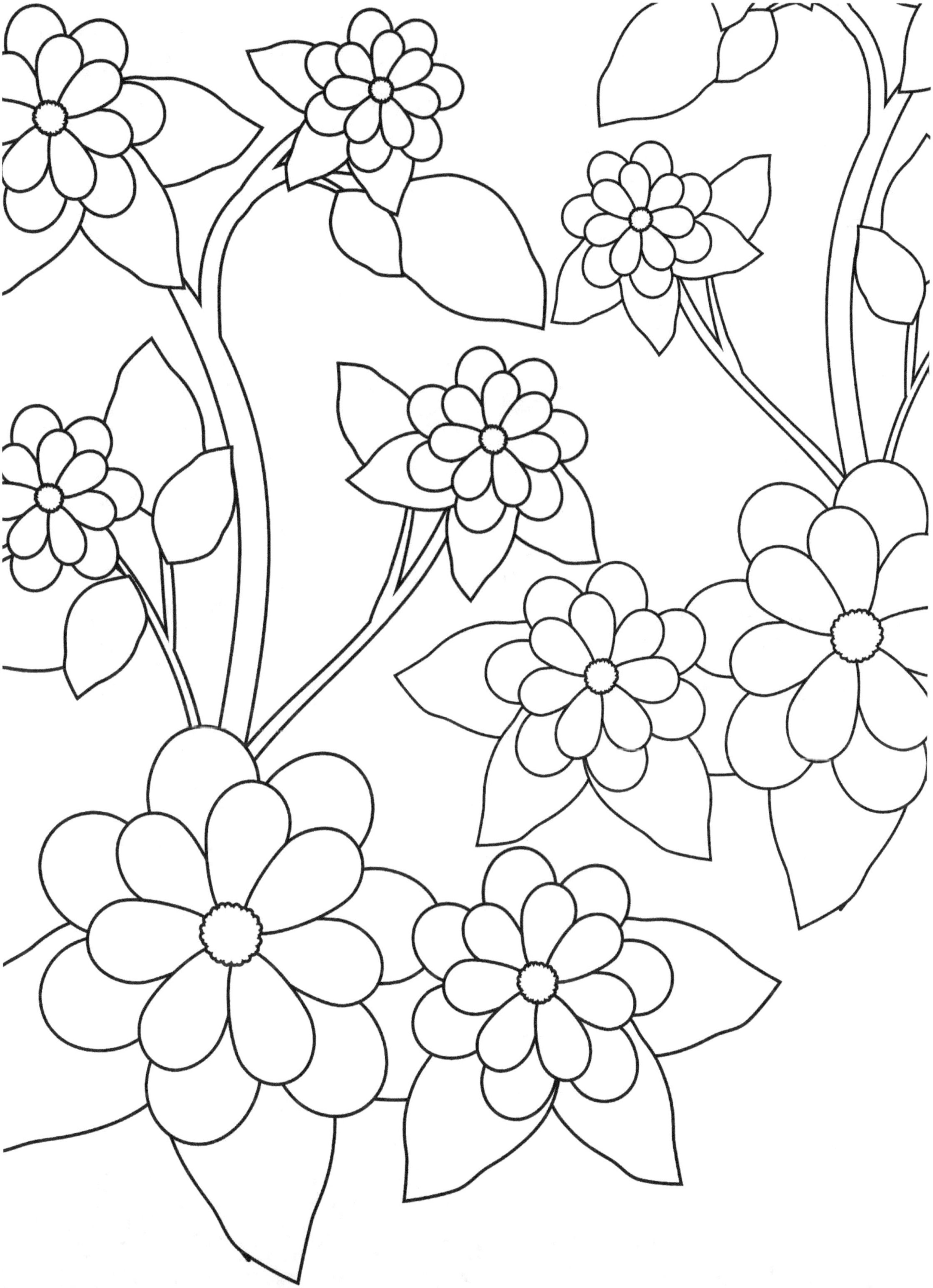

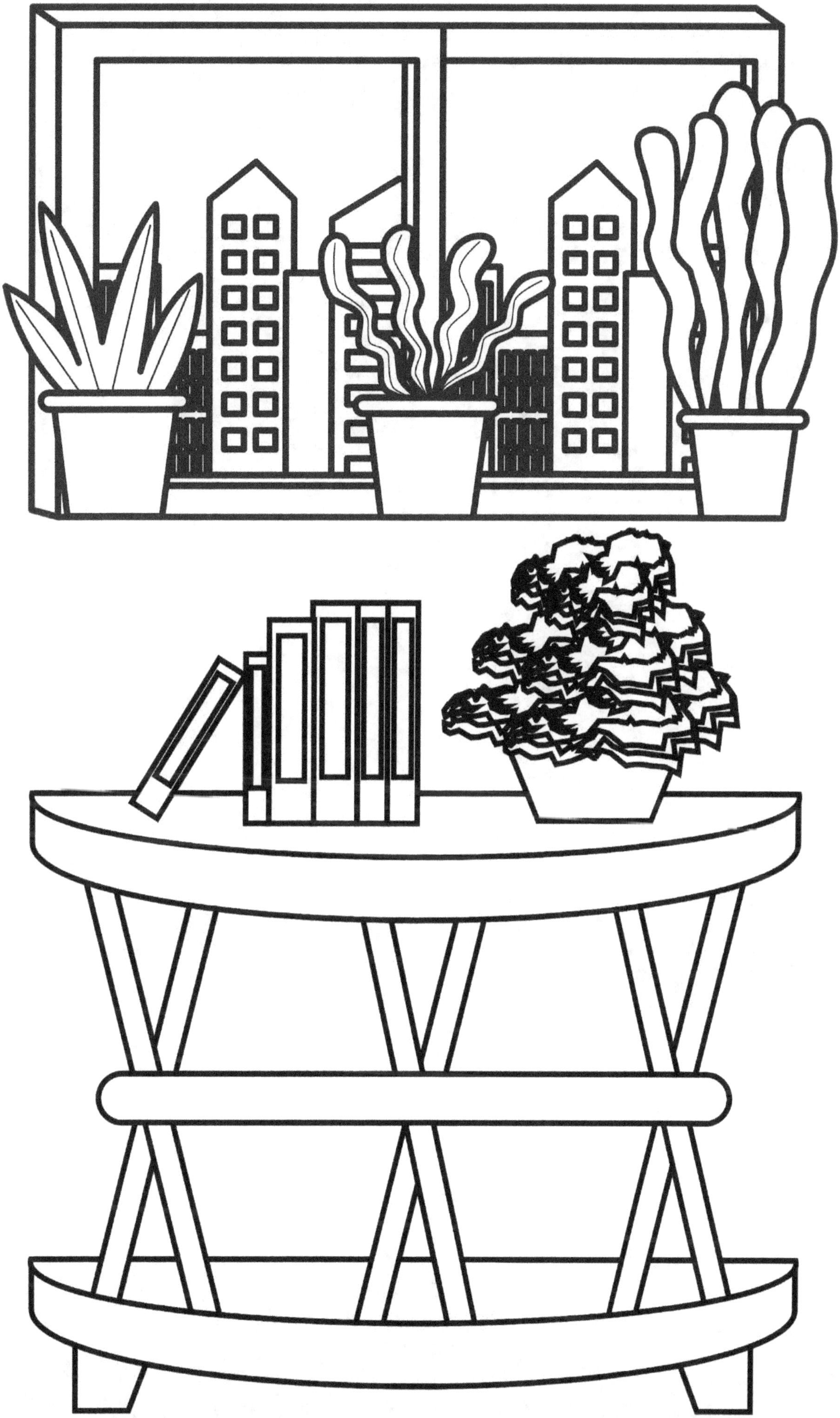

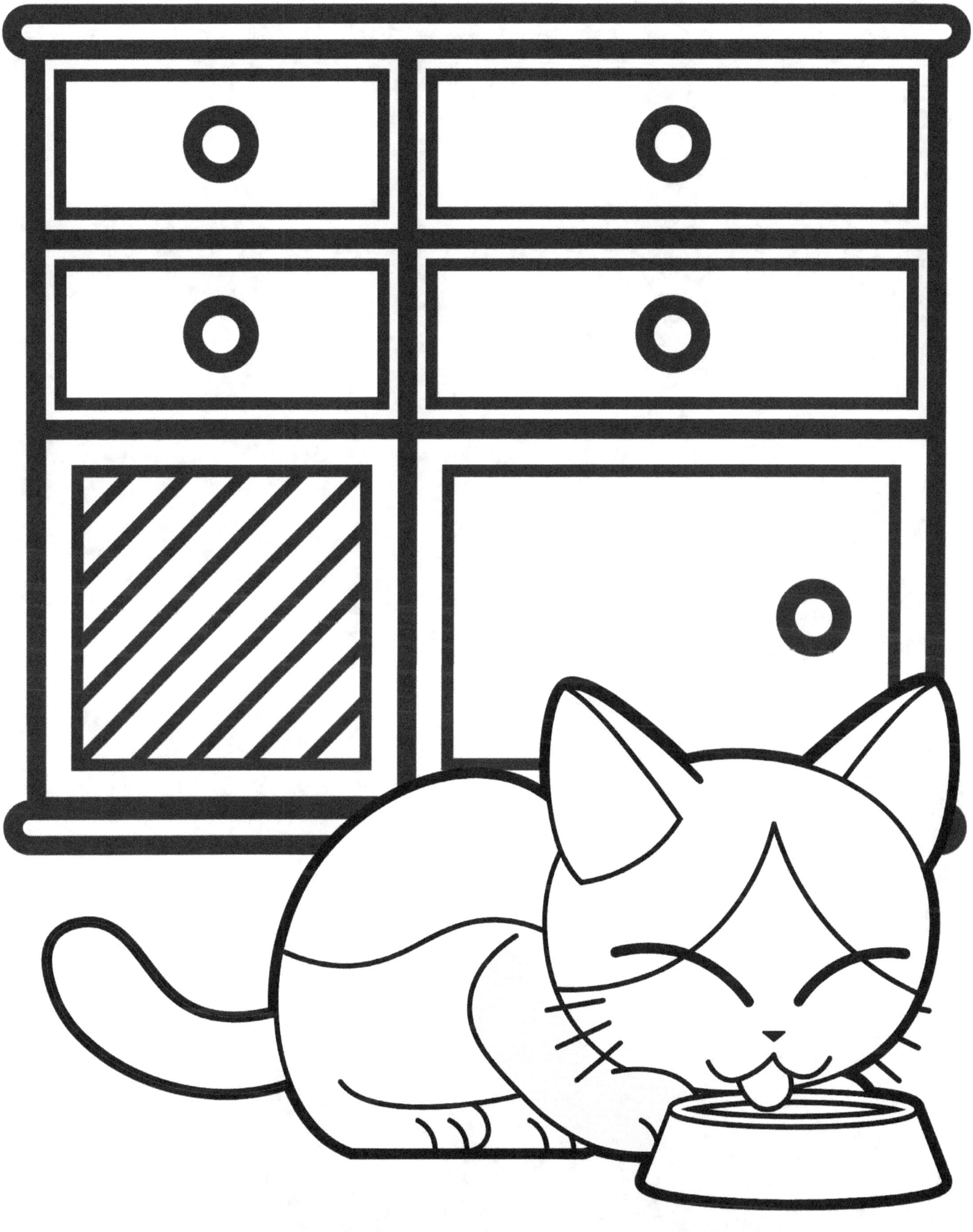

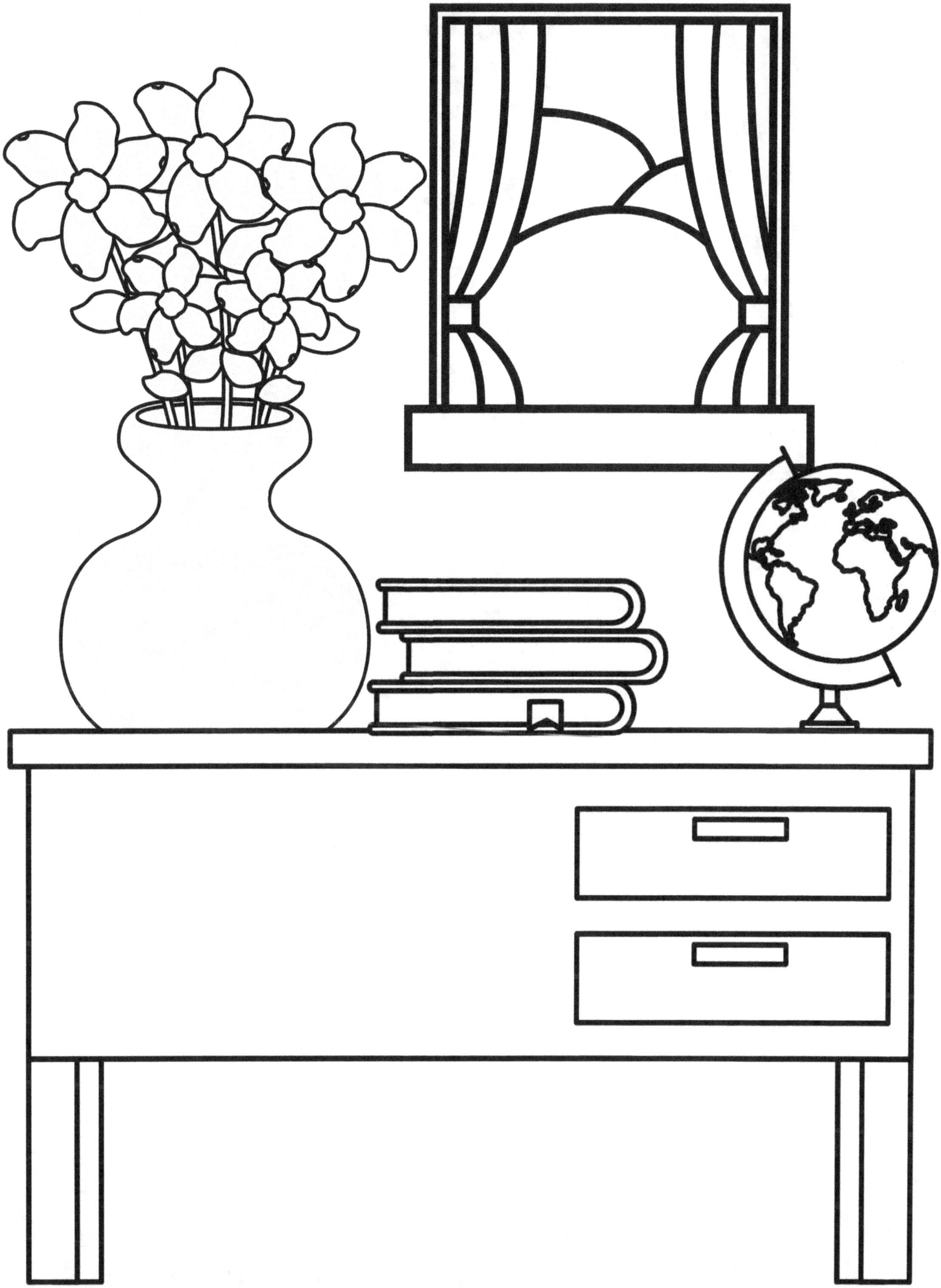

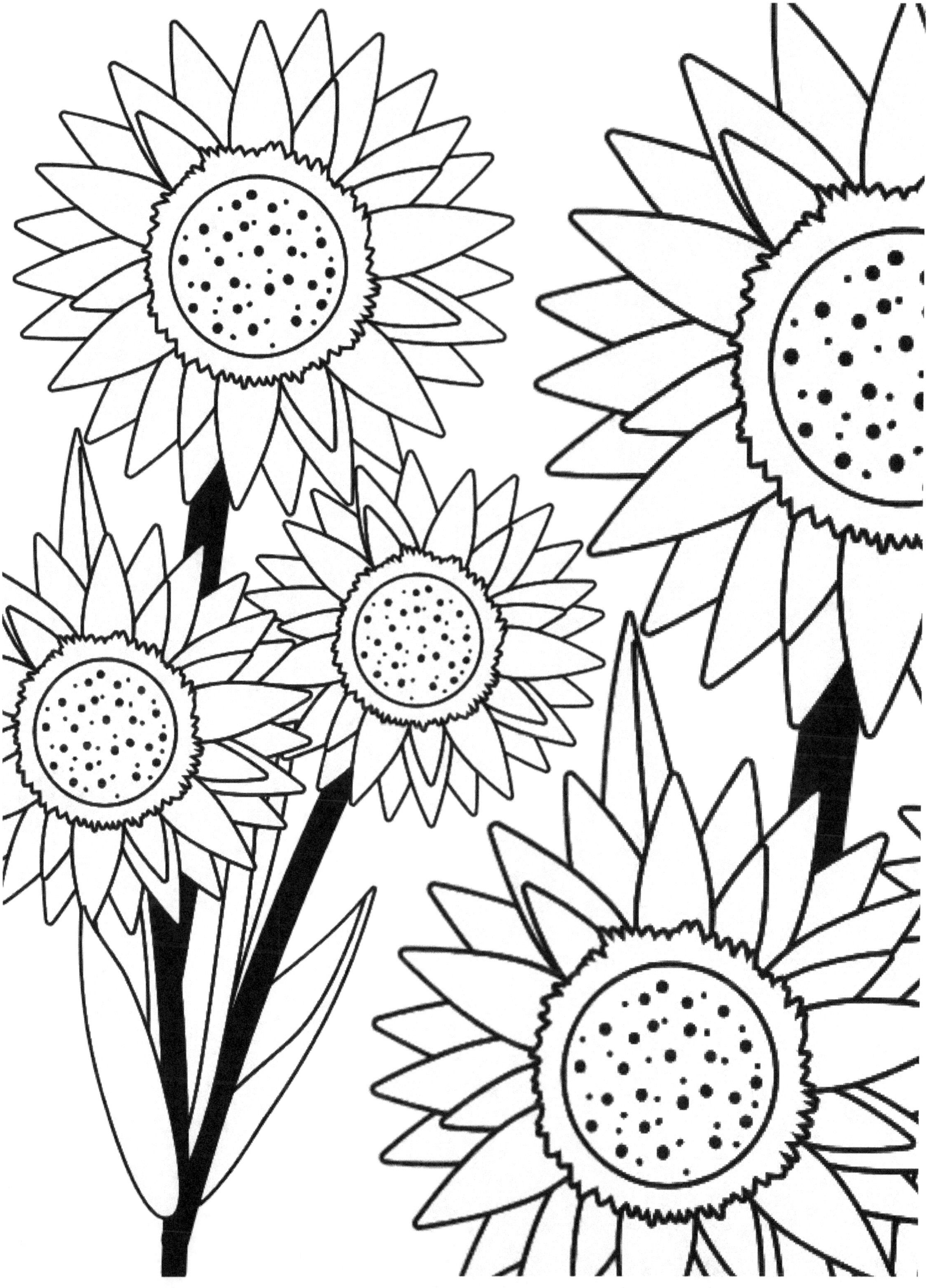

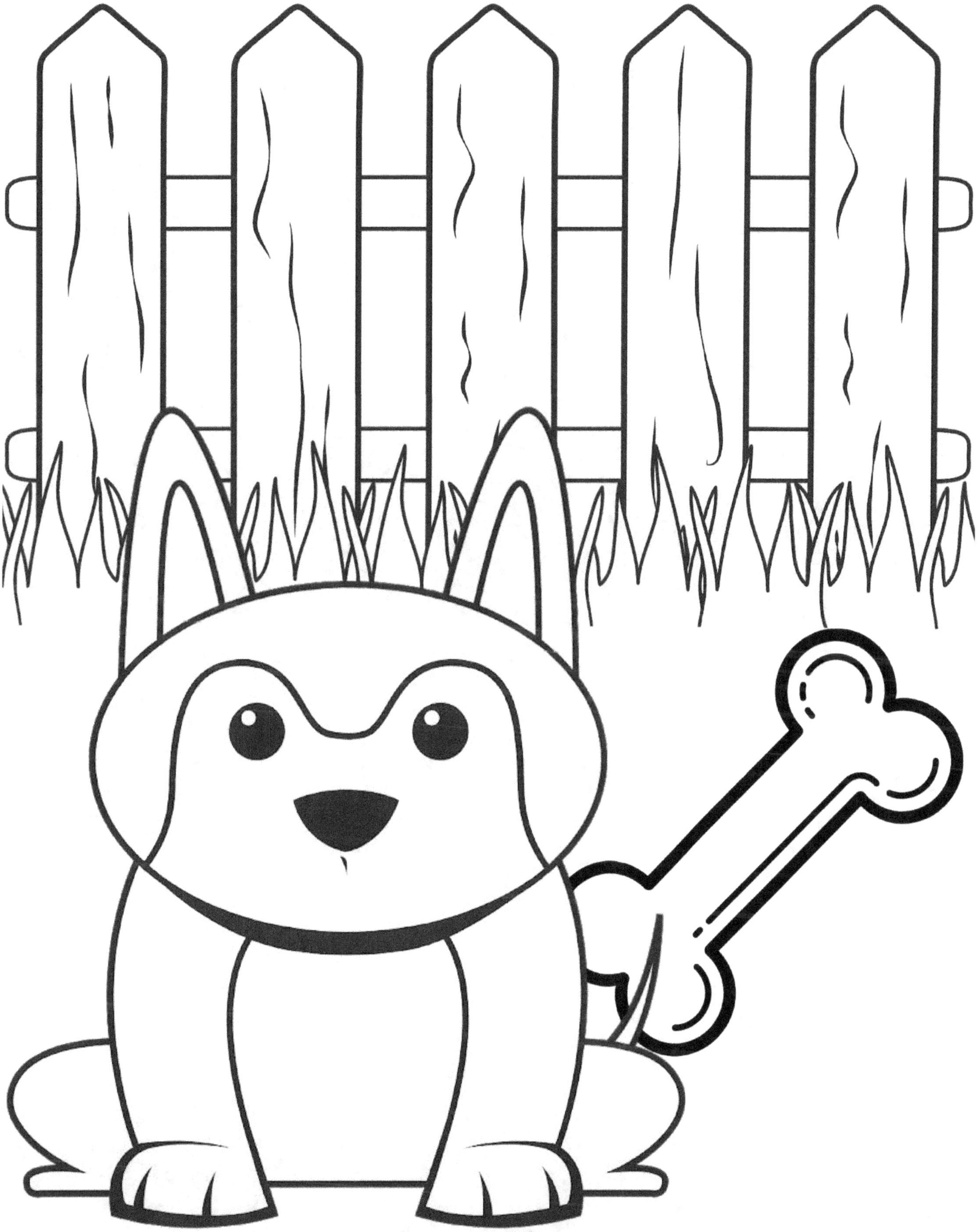

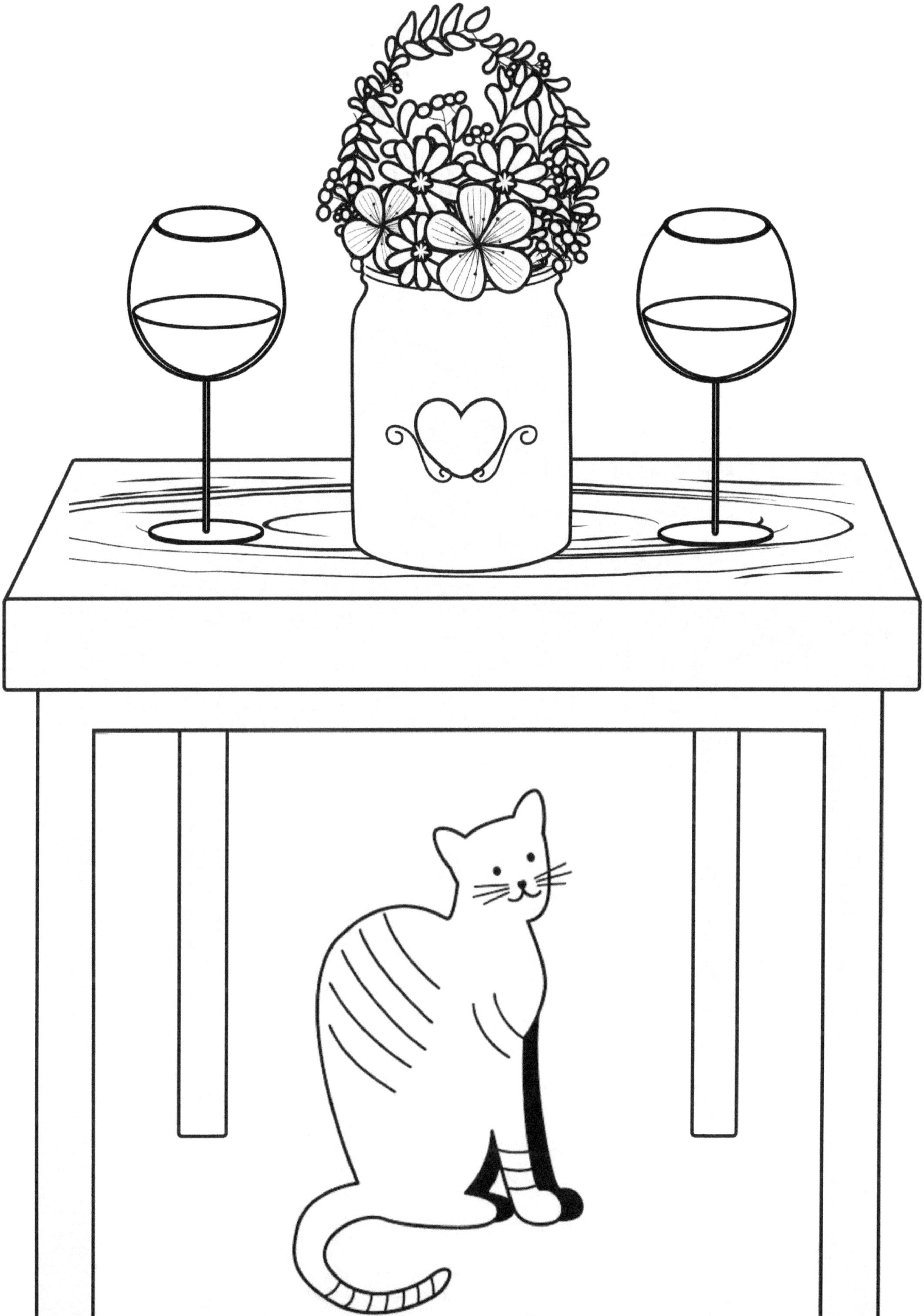

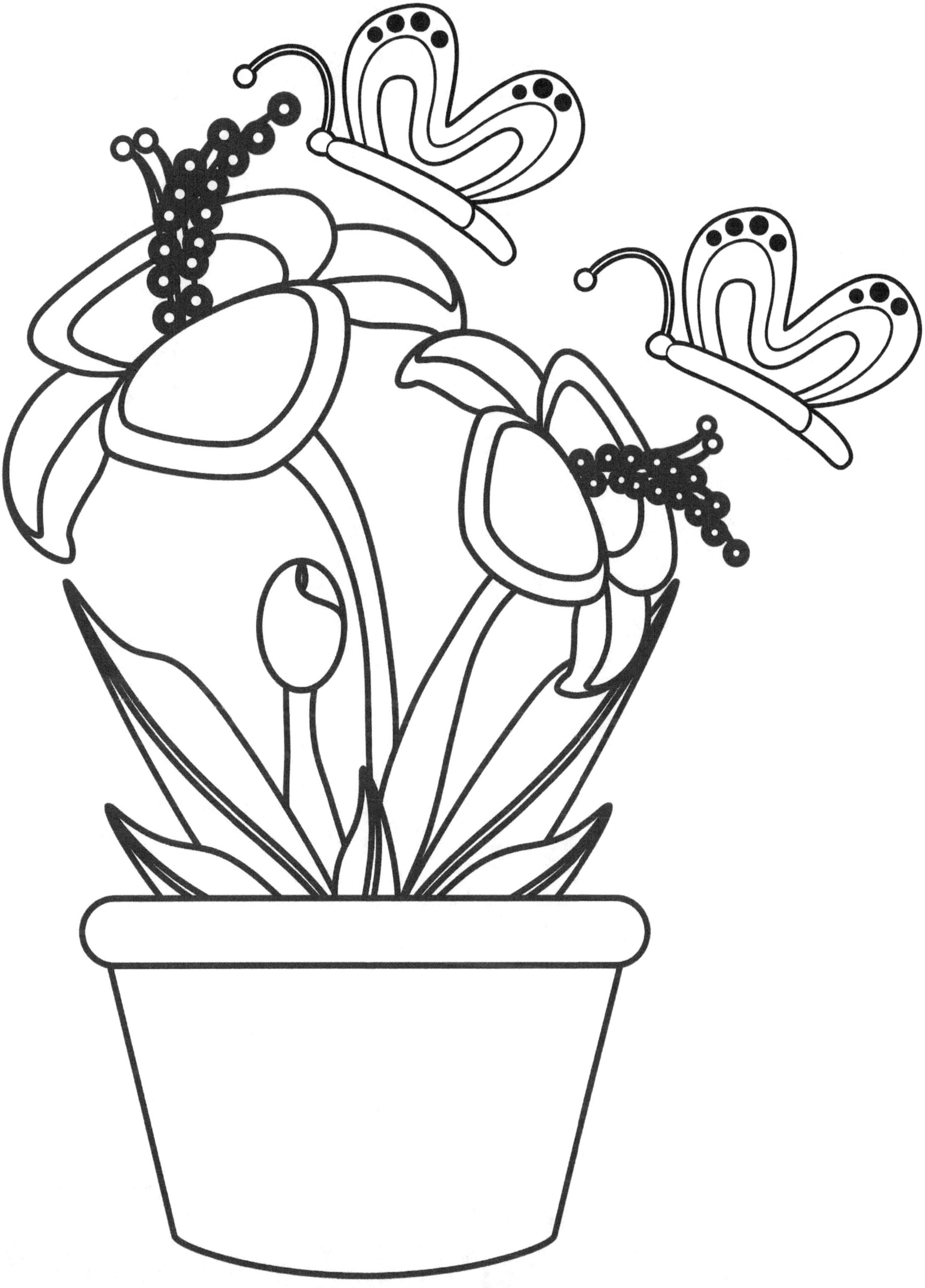

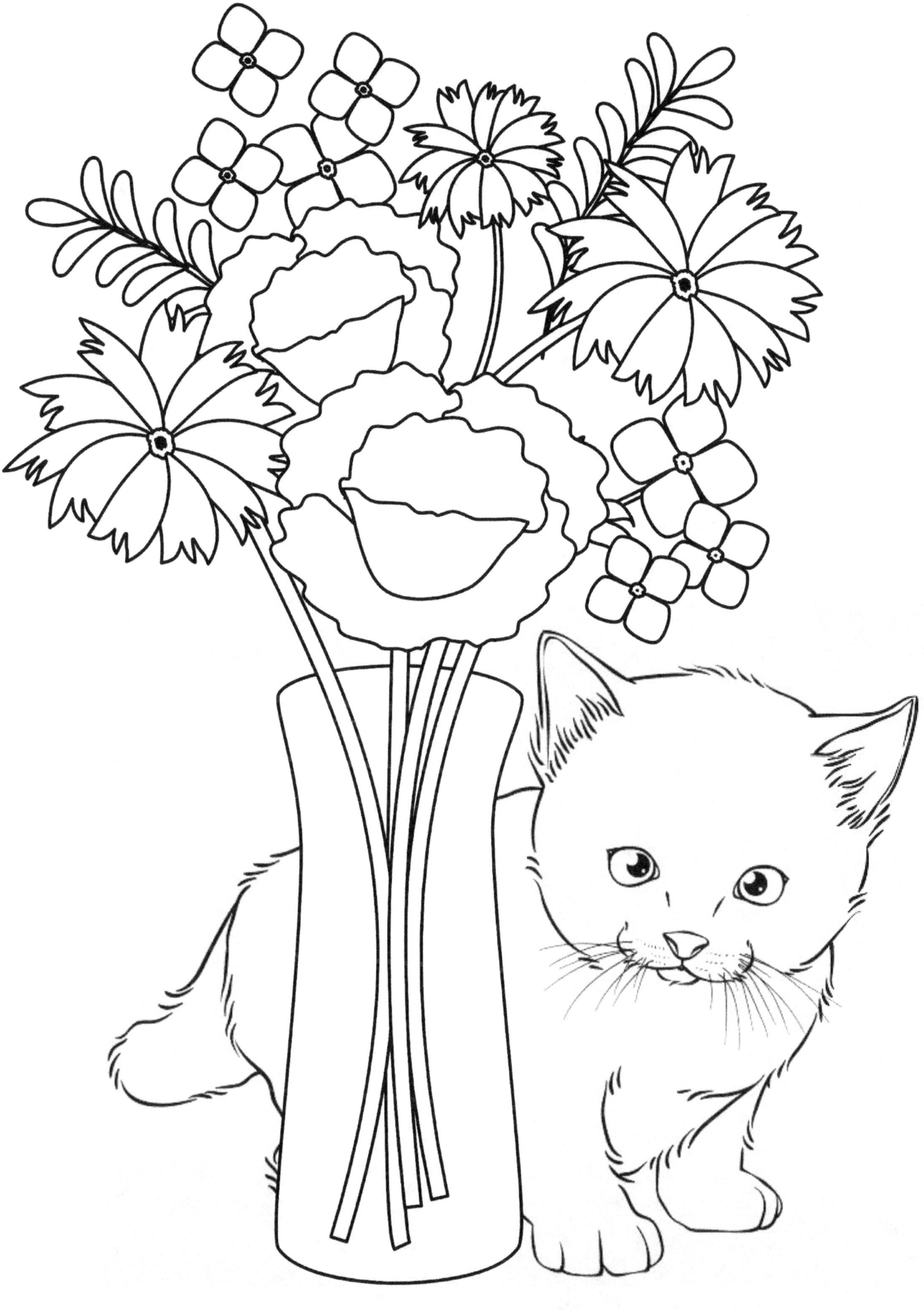

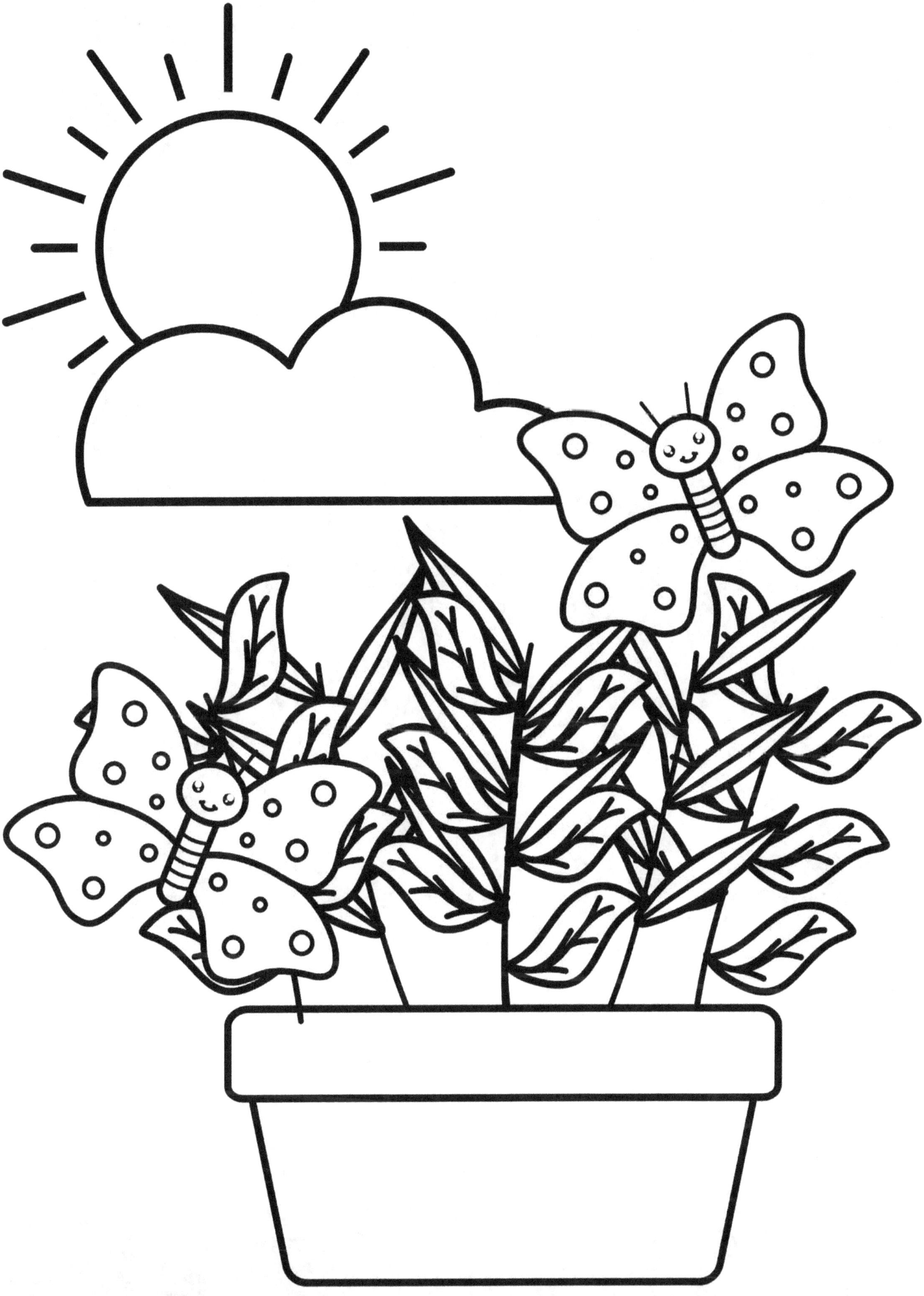

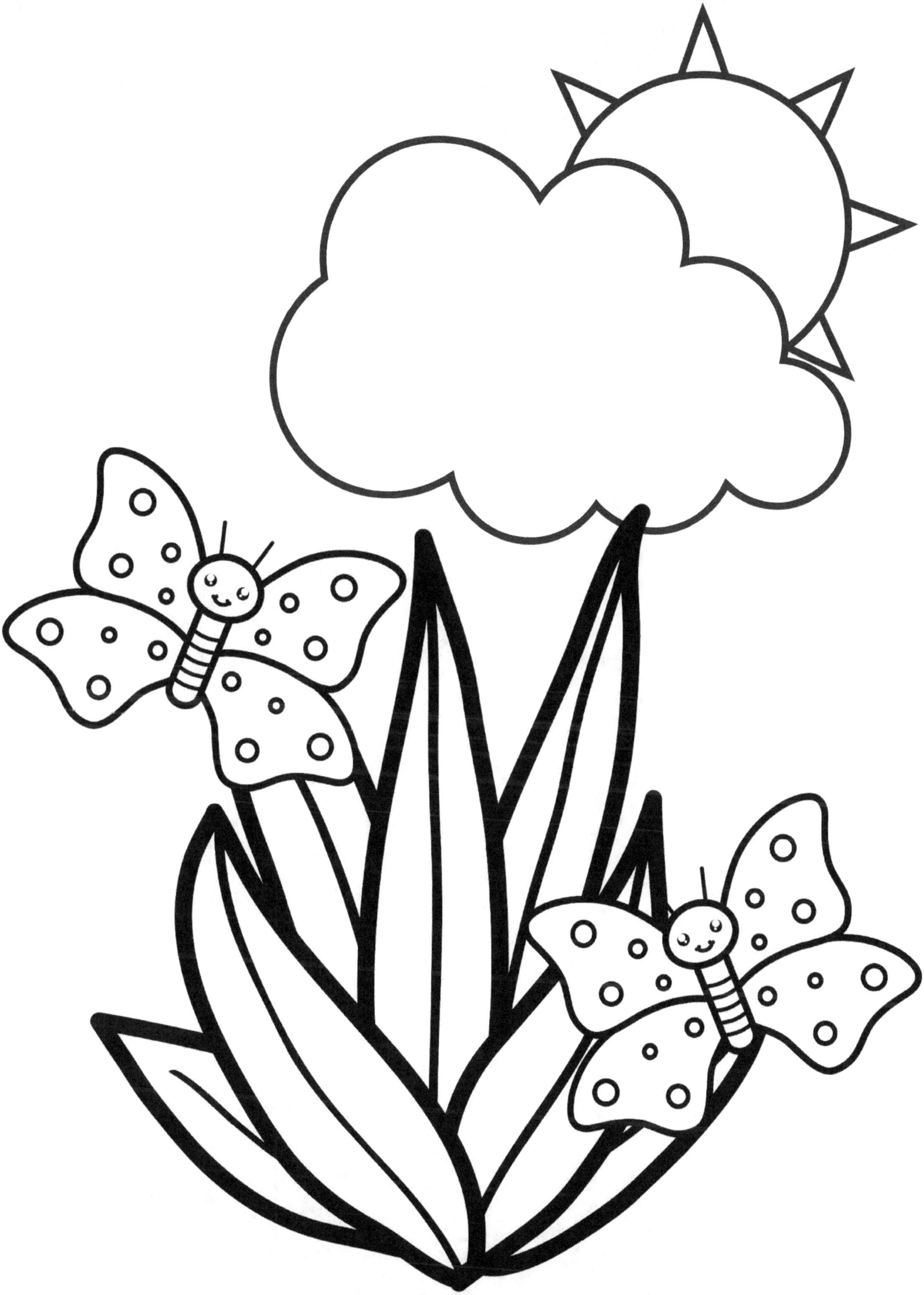

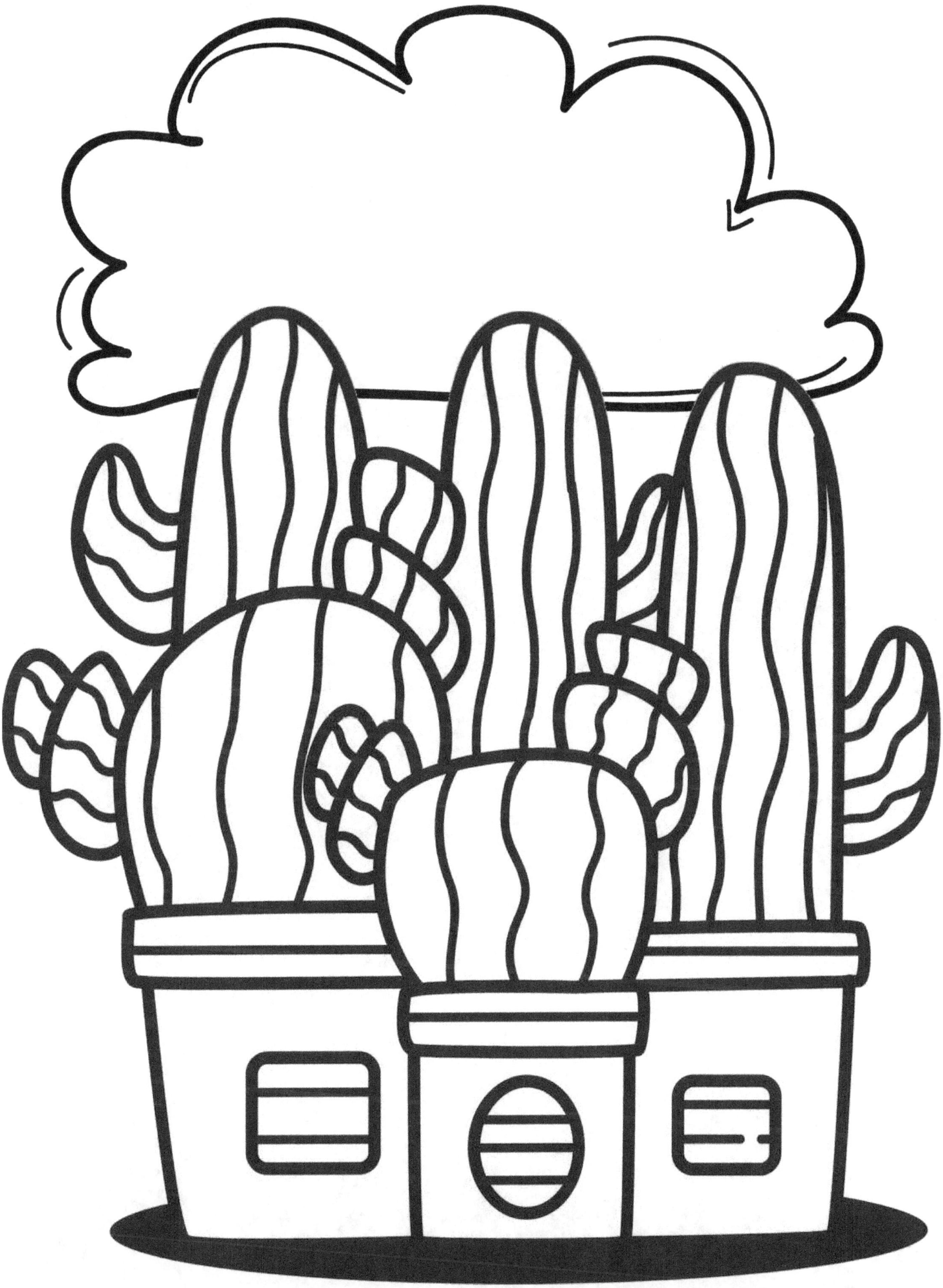

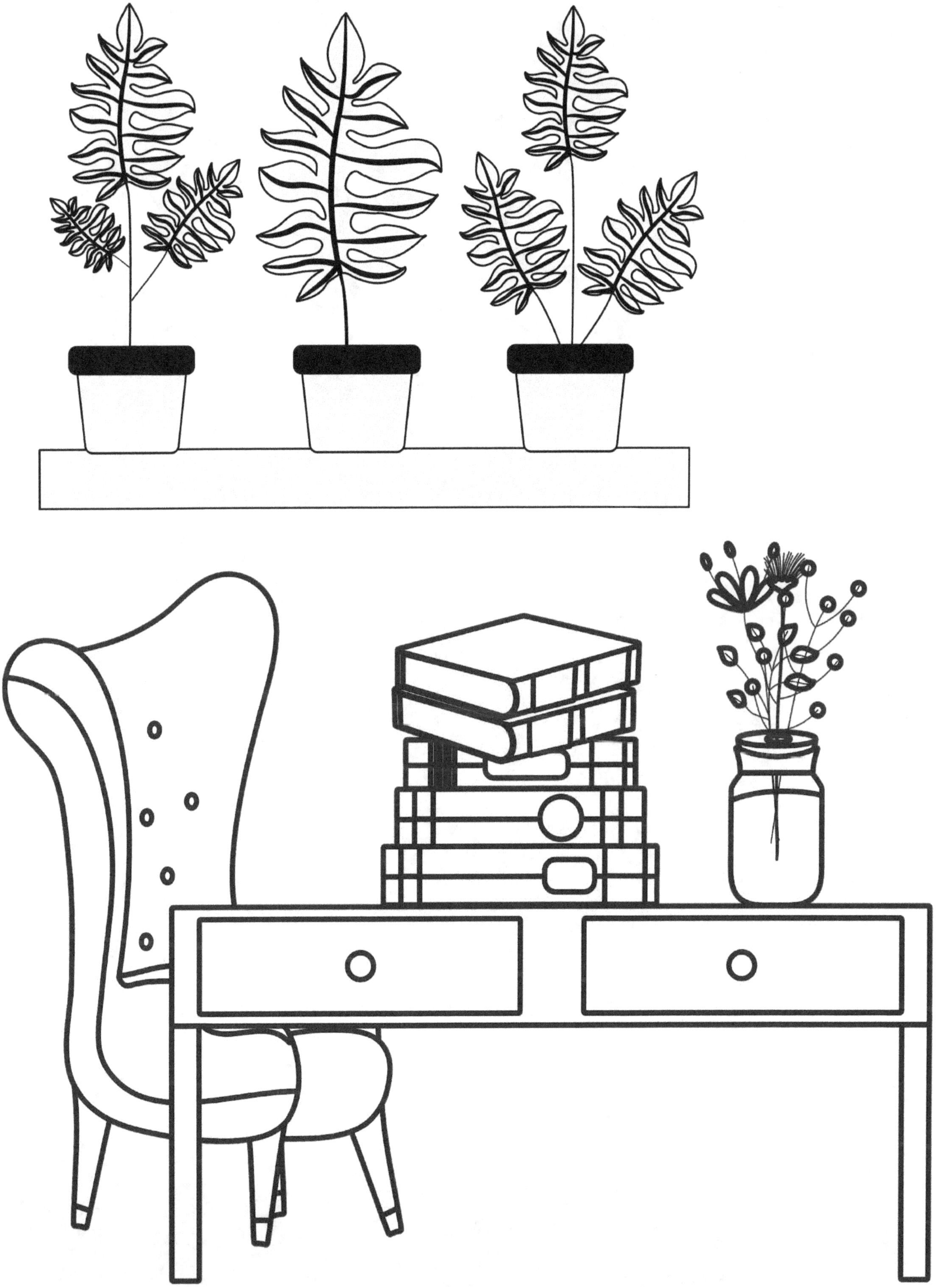

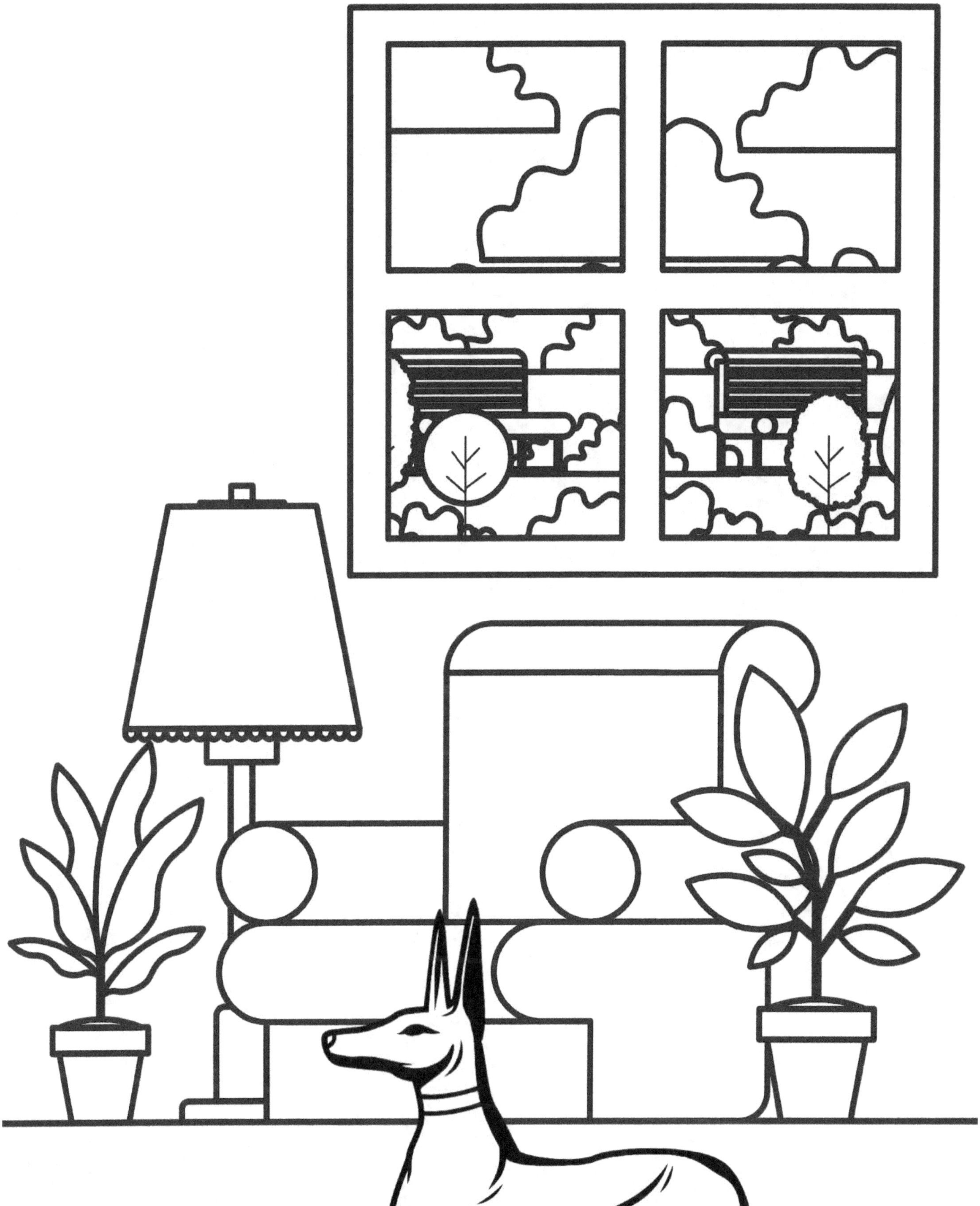

www.ingramcontent.com/pod-product-compliance
Lightning Source LLC
Chambersburg PA
CBHW080853220526
45467CB00008B/2496
9798691650123